INITIATION

INITIATION

The Spiritual Transformation of the Experiencer

A Guide for Contact Experiencers

REV. MICHAEL JS CARTER

Acme, Nadir, Fulcrum & Pivot, Ltd.

Contents

A Story   1

INTRODUCTION

PART ONE: FOUNDATION

One   The Initiation Begins   12

Two   The Indicators   25

Three   The Separation   36

Four   The Teachers and Mentors   44

Five   The Trials, Disciplines and Vows   52

Six   Cultural Traditions and Research   58

Seven   The Children   65

Eight Wrapping it Up 69

PART TWO: TRANSFORMATION

Nine The Spiritual Transformation 78

Ten In Their Own Words: Experiencer
Stories 88

Appendix A 125
Appendix B 126
Appendix C 127
Acknowledgements 128
About the Author 129

A Story

There is an old Hindu legend that tells of a time when all human beings were gods and goddesses, but they so abused their divinity that Brahma, the supreme god, decided to take it away from human beings and to hide it where they would never find it. The question became where exactly to hide this divinity from them.

The lesser deities were called to a council to consider this question. Some suggested burying human divinity deep into the earth, for they would never think to look there. But Brahma said, "No, that would never do, for eventually they would dig deep into the earth and find it."

Other deities suggested that we sink this divinity into the deepest ocean and hide it there. Yet again, Brahma replied, "No, not there, for humans will eventually learn to dive into the deepest waters and will find it there." Another deity suggested that this divinity should be taken to the highest mountaintop and hide it there. But again, Brahma said, "No, for human beings will eventually learn to climb every mountaintop on earth and take their divinity up again."

Finally, the lesser deities gave up and concluded, " We do not know where to hide it, for it appears that there is no place on earth or in the sea that human beings will not eventually reach. But then Brahma came up with an idea. He said this is what we will do with the divinity of humanity. "We will hide it deep within human beings, for they will never, ever think to look for it there."

Ever since that time, the legend tells us, human beings have been searching all over the earth, searching up and down, climbing, digging, diving, exploring, searching for something that can only be found within. Approximately, a man named Yeshua discovered the secret and attempted to share it with the world, but human beings would not listen. Other messengers, other saints, sages, prophets, and avatars have tried to remind us of our divinity by delivering this message throughout recorded history, but it fell on deaf ears. Unfortunately, the divinity of human beings remains the best-kept secret in the entire world.

Introduction

May you live in interesting times.
- Chinese Proverb

Those of you who have been studying and report-
ing about UFOs for a long time, I can say to you now,
all along, you were right.
- Luis Elizondo, Director of Global Security & Special Programs,
Former Director of Advanced Aerospace Threat Identification Program

Like it or not, we live in interesting times. These
are times of danger, uncertainty, and unrest. Difficult
times also tend to be times of heightened creativity,
so I have hope. Human beings have recently passed
from 2,000 years of the old *Piscean Age* and into the
new *Age of Aquarius.* During the Piscean Age, the
world needed a savior, and the world's major religions
reflected that. For two millennia, Christianity told us
that we were born in sin, and we needed religious leaders to show us how to live. People worldwide seemed
to need this sacred guidance, and there is profound

and much-needed truth and beauty to those teachings.

The next 2,000 years, The *Age of Aquarius,* offers humanity the possibility of creating a more peaceful and harmonious existence with each other and the planet. A change in consciousness is required to reveal the truth that resides within each one of us. This new consciousness is lying dormant within us. Some may call it *Buddha Consciousness;* some may refer to it as *God Consciousness,* Christ *Consciousness, Cosmic Consciousness, The Universal Mind,* or the *Primal Cause.* Behind this is an energy or energetic being that many call God. Call it what you will; the label doesn't matter. What does matter is that a new world is being born. The sign of Aquarius is the sign of the "information bearer." We are surrounded now by so much information that it can feel overwhelming. The key is discernment. Critical thinking is needed to wade through the sea of information and data to discern what is helpful in the service of all beings. What information do we need to be of service to ourselves and our world?

In short, the age of humanity needing a "savior" has given way to the change in consciousness where 'we are the ones we have been waiting for.' The time is ripe to mature as a collective species and address the increasingly urgent needs of each other and our planet. To be clear, the *Age of Aquarius* does not mean that humanity will bend to the words of the prophet Isaiah, beat our swords into plowshares and join hands in singing Kumbaya. It means that we have an opportunity now to do the good work, develop a shift in our perceptions, then move past the attitudes of fear and aggression that maintain the illusion that we are all separate from each other. The choice is up to each one of us.

I perceive this shift in consciousness happening all over the world at this time; humanity's struggle to be free, to create a more just and equitable world. I see a hunger for transforming a world from competitive to cooperative. I also see the forces of the status-quo fighting tooth and nail to maintain the profitable disharmony of fear, greed, and militarism. The possibilities for us to annihilate each other and our planet are numerous. And yet, there are artists, healers, politicians, philosophers, and many others who indeed envision a new world, a world of peace, justice, and love.

Experiencers, Contactees, and Abductees
Amongst those people who envision this new world are those who are called "*Experiencers.*" Experiencers were known back in the 1950s and '60s, as "*Contactees.*" They are people who say they have had contact with extraterrestrials or "off-world intelligences". When I was in New York City in the 1990s, after my own experiences, people who claimed they were kidnapped and taken aboard UFOs were called "Abductees". As an Experiencer, I have had many contacts with these "off-world intelligences." The word

"abductee" always bothered me. I felt that the word implied a sinister, nefarious intent or experience. I now prefer the term *"Experiencer"* as it is more open and confers more agency in describing the experience.

Who are these "Experiencers" making these out-landish claims of being visited by people from outer space? Experiencers come from all walks of life, and it appears that the Star People do not discriminate. All ages, races, socio-economic classes-they come from all demographics. Although the majority of reports are from white people, people of color are also Experi-encers.

Most of these encounters are individual. By this, I mean that a person may encounter a Star Person while around other people who don't participate or even know about it. For example, I was the Experi-encer more than once as my partner was asleep in the same bed but did not see anything or even wake up. Perhaps she somehow could not awaken while this was happening because the Star People did not want her to. I don't know. Some people recall being taken into a ship after these bedroom encounters. I did not remember being taken aboard a craft until the late Dr. Jean Mundy hypnotically regressed me.

Not all contact experiences occur at night, as they do in the movies. Experiencer stories are full of ac-counts of people having contacts in broad daylight, but usually in isolated or remote areas. And of course, there also are stories of multiple witnesses having a group contact experience.

I allow those who have shared such experiences to label them as they see fit. My intent is not to quibble over labels or to tell others how to interpret their unique experiences. However, my purpose here is twofold. First of all, many people who have had contact have not felt kidnapped or abducted. These are not words or descriptions that they are comfortable using. Secondly, many people (myself included) view their contact experiences as ultimately positive, leading to a significant **Spiritual Transformation**, despite the confusion and trauma they may have experienced. I see it as an *initiation* into a new and profound way of being in the world. It can initiate a shift in consciousness and worldview from fear and lack-based to love and connectedness-based.

As Thomas James Streicher, Ph.D. points out in his book, *Extra-Planetary Experiences; Alien-Human Contact and the Expansion of Consciousness*, we are continually being told what to do, feel, and think, and who to be. We have lost our perspective and our sense of place in the greater Universe. We forget that we are own masters and the most vital expert in our life. As we come to know life beyond our Earth, we must acknowledge the limitations of our science and its worldview and our religions and their worldview. All of that must shift and change. That is enough to trigger panic in many of us, who are already stressed and fearful of change. We cling to our particular filters through which we comprehend our world. So necessarily, this process of awakening will happen slowly, and only for those who are ready. As we begin to acknowledge extraterrestrial life, perennial questions arise about our place in the cosmos and how we define it. If confirmed tomorrow, how would the presence of extraterrestrials affect your own self-image?

At the beginning of this book, the quote by Mr. Elizondo gives me a sense of vindication, I know I am not alone. I must say that I do not see these Star People as a threat. Yet after all of the shame and ridicule, after hiding what I was going through for so long, even after therapy and the discovery that I was not crazy, it still felt good to read that he had said, "...you were right all along." That's what I am saying to all of you Experiencers out there with the writing of this book.

As I write this, the United States Government and its military are finally (although begrudgingly) acknowledging that there are UFOs, or as they continue to refer to the craft as Unidentified Arial Phenomena in our skies. Of course, the military and other government intelligence agencies are beginning to also speak of these events as "national security threats." That is disturbing but understandable. When the only tool you have is a hammer, everything looks like a nail. What we don't understand, we fear, and fear has brought us to the violent place we are today. Hopefully, cooler heads will prevail, and perhaps we can see this not as a threat but as an opportunity to learn and grow. We as Experiencers, may help shift worldwide perceptions from fear to curiosity about this Universe and our place in it. We shall see.

In these exciting and challenging times, the Experiencer can be a harbinger of truth, the truth that we are not alone in this Universe and multiverse and never have been. Perhaps a shift in consciousness is needed to move beyond nationality and nation-states into "galactic citizens" with a planetary future filled with more possibilities than we could ever imagine. The Experiencers and their stories may be a key to help unlock this future so that the world we are waiting for can someday finally become--- the world attained.

Rev. Michael J S Carter
Asheville, North Carolina, May 2021

PART ONE: Foundation

Chapter One

The Initiation Begins

There are more things in heaven and earth Horatio, than are dreamt of in your philosophy.
- Hamlet, by William Shakespeare

At the outset, I want to state that I am an ordained member of the professional clergy. I am seminary trained. I am a member of the Unitarian Universalist denomination, and I serve a U.U. congregation. My theology is liberal and is the lens through which I view spirituality and religion. Now, let us move on. I will share my initial adult contact experience with you. As a young child, I had many instances of what can be only labeled "high strangeness" but the story that I am about to relate left no doubt about what was going on.

It was December 28, 1989. I had just returned from a wonderful ten-day trip to Mexico where my girlfriend and I had visited the Mayan Pyramids at Tulum and Chichen-Itza. It felt good to get back to our apartment on the Upper West Side of Manhattan and back to our daily routine.

Later that day, I attended a party in the "Hell's Kitchen" section of Manhattan despite the freezing temperatures. I wanted to show off my tan, talk about the trip a bit, and didn't plan to stay long. I just wanted to make an appearance and get back home. When I arrived, I chatted with a few people and ate some snacks but no alcohol as I was quite fatigued. I left the party after about 90 minutes and caught the subway back uptown to get home. It was so nice to be in my warm apartment, and my own bed; my girlfriend and I called it a night around 11:30 pm. During the early morning hours (and to this very day, I don't know why), for some reason, I felt as though I had to get up. I don't recall having to go to the bathroom or anything like that and I really didn't want to get out of my warm bed.

I usually sleep on my stomach, and there was this persistent feeling that I must open my eyes and get up. Perhaps I felt a presence in the room, but when I rolled over and looked at the foot of my bed, nothing could have prepared me for what I saw. I have never been so frightened in my entire life! At the foot of the bed was an individual, chalk-white in complexion, no more than 3-4 feet tall, with a spindly body dressed in a tight-fitting jumpsuit that looked like aluminum foil. It was made of extremely silvery and shiny material. His (at least I thought the individual was male but didn't know for sure) head was huge, and his eyes were a deep black and very large and appeared to wrap around his head.

There was a cobalt blue light around him, and surrounding that light was an extremely bright white light like part of his aura or energy field, and he just stared at me. I stared back but felt as if my heart was going to jump out of my chest. At that moment, I did what any self-respecting male would do---I pulled the covers over my head and hoped he would go away! My girlfriend either would not or could not wake up and I was terrified. Suddenly, there was a whooshing sound in my ears as if I was engulfed in a windstorm. The temperature changed drastically, and it felt as if I had left the room and was outside. I was freezing. Now I must mention that at the time, I lived on the 15th floor of a residential hotel on the Upper West Side of Manhattan, in the city that never sleeps.

Just as suddenly, the sound of wind had stopped, and I was warm again. I summoned the courage to pull the covers down from my head to see where I was and more importantly, to see where *he* was, but there was simply complete silence. An eerie quiet was all that remained, and my girlfriend had not even stirred! I attempted to wake her, but she wouldn't (or couldn't) wake up. I checked to see that she was still breathing, and thank goodness she was, but I couldn't wake her. Eventually, she woke, and we spoke about what happened. These visits continued for eight months or so on every full and new moon.

Eventually, I attended a support group called S.P.A.C.E. (Search Project for Aspects of Close Encounters). The group was created and facilitated by Mr. Harold Walter Egeln in March of 1992, and Mr. Egeln is also an Experiencer. The late Jean Mundy hypnotically regressed me within weeks after the experience. A few years later, the late Budd Hopkins regressed me after speaking at a U.F.O. Conference in Long Island, NY.

I credit both Dr. Mundy and Budd Hopkins for helping me to come to grips with what was happening. It took me nearly 20 years to learn to sleep with the lights out again, and to be truthful; there are still nights where I will keep the lights on until the very last minute before turning them off to go to sleep. In the early days, during the visits by the "Grays," I was shown past lives as well and was encouraged to pray and to study energy healing, particularly hands-on Reiki healing. I was shown this telepathically.

There were also times when several years would go by between our face-to-face contacts, and despite the terror experienced during these contacts, I would long to see them again as I had truly missed the visits. Sometimes, I would even see them in my "third eye" while meditating. I longed for the next time I would see them face to face despite the intense fear it would cause.

Another visit stands out to me. On July 4, 2013, at 9:50 pm E.S.T., an extraterrestrial Nordic Person healed a blood clot in my right leg by shooting an apple green beam out of his right hand into my stomach area. I did not have a medical history of blood clots, nor had I ever had a blood clot before. Nor have I had one since. At the beginning of the year 2013, I was going through a rough time in my life. I was getting a divorce from my second marriage, and my dad had just died from pancreatic cancer. In addition, the new administration at the hospital where I worked had decided to "clean house," so I was about to lose my job as a chaplain.

I suddenly developed swelling in my right leg from my ankle to the groin area. The pain was excruciating, I could barely touch my leg without feeling pain. A close friend suggested that I get it checked out, but of course, being stubborn, I refused. I thought that perhaps I had pulled a muscle and that it would heal on its own. The pain was so great that I finally took my friend's advice and called my primary care physician, who saw me later that day. After looking at my leg, he asked me if I had driven to his office alone or if a friend had driven me. I replied that I drove myself. He strongly suggested that I get myself to the hospital for an ultrasound as soon as possible because he said, "you have a blood clot that is so huge that if it burst, it would be life-threatening." I did as he told me.

The doctors at the hospital seemed alarmed, which only frightened me even more. Upon discharge, they told me that I needed to begin taking Coumadin immediately and that I also had to start injecting myself in the stomach with a drug called Enoxaparin to thin the blood so the clot would not travel to my lungs or brain.

So on the evening of July 4, 2013, I was lying in bed resting a bit. My daughter, my ex-wife, and I had attended the annual July 4 celebrations in Asheville for seven years, and finally, in the year 2013, I caught a break. Thunderstorms rained out the gathering on that holiday evening, and I was relieved because I do not enjoy fireworks, and the event was tedious for me. Yet, I wanted to be a good dad and a good ex-spouse, so I went along with this for seven long years.

So that night, I was home listening to the thunder, and the rain was coming down in buckets. I have quite a few friends who fought in the Vietnam War, and they would tell me how they would have to learn to sleep out in the rain if they were out on patrol, or a night ambush or in their foxholes, even in a thunderstorm. They said they just got used to it; even if artillery was firing, they simply endured.

The thunder was so loud that evening I began thinking of what they had dealt with (mind you, I was thinking of all this while in the comfort of my apartment) when suddenly the energy in my bedroom changed. That's the only way I can explain it. It was as if the air had changed 'texture.' It sounded as if the rain had stopped as well, but something was different in my room. I was lying on my stomach facing away from my bedroom door, and when I turned around, there was a very pale-looking man standing at my bedroom door. He was blond-haired and very muscular, with a monk's cowl on his head. It looked like a "hoodie," only it was a full-length robe. He was well over six feet tall as his head was only a few inches from the ceiling.

We just stared at each other for a moment, and I felt that my heart would come through my chest. The tall, thin being extended his hand, then an apple-green light went out of his palm and hit me in the stomach. I did not feel a thing when the light hit me, and then he just disappeared. The particles of his body somehow dispersed, and there was nothing left.

I looked at my stomach and saw nothing, but the blood clot was gone when I looked at my right leg. My right leg, which had been twice the size of my left leg was now its normal size. I called a friend in California to tell him what had happened, but it was only around 7 pm there, so no one picked up. I left a voice message and hoped he would call back. I had so much energy surging through my body that I felt as if I could spring around the apartment complex. The following day I showed my leg to my daughter and my ex-wife, and they were astounded. They were so excited and happy for me, they both said, "They healed your leg!" This story can also be found in the book, *The Healing Power of U.F.O.s by* Preston Dennett.

Now the fun part was figuring out how to explain to my doctor what had happened. No, I did not tell the doctors exactly what had happened. They were pretty curious as to how suddenly the clot dissolved after weeks of blood thinners and treatment. They would not let the matter drop and kept pressing me with questions about how the leg healed so quickly. Finally, I just said that I didn't know but can you just be happy for me? This question seemed to put them on the defensive, and they backed off, saying, of course, they were pleased. They wanted me to return to health. I believed they did, but these are people of science, and they could not understand that some things occur in our world that science cannot explain, especially in the realm of healing.

These are just two examples of the many experiences I have had with non-human off-world intelligences, and I must tell you truthfully that I would not trade them for anything in the world, despite my fear during the events. I have also had the experiences of meeting Reptilians, Arcturians, and Praying Mantis beings, all of whom would at various times find their way to my bedroom. I know these contact experiences will continue, and I look forward to it.

After a while, the fear did eventually subside somewhat, it took about about 20 years, though. Before then, I would not turn off my bedroom light until I was sure that I was ready to drop off to sleep. I felt that I would not get a visitation as long as I had the light on. No, it was not rational, but that was part of my post-trauma. Honestly, even to this day, I do feel a little fear, but nothing untoward has happened to me during all of those years of contact, at least not intentionally. It is not so much the bizarre appearance these people have, but the suddenness they can appear at my bedside that is frightening. One moment I am alone, and then I'm not! There is also partial paralysis, where I cannot move but can breathe, hear, and see what is going on. I don't know if the paralysis is for their protection or mine. These situations, being helpless, can be terribly frightening.

And yet, gradually, like a large glacier beginning to melt, I began to soften, to evolve. Then I began to realize on a deep level that these people meant me no harm and that it was my fear of them, my fear of the unknown, indeed my fear of life itself, that was causing all of the alarm and anxiety in me. I was evolving and beginning to question the other events and times when I let fear control my emotions and affect my decisions. Today, I consider these contacts to be positive experiences, and they did accelerate my spiritual growth by leaps and bounds. A few illustrations may be in order.

First of all, my theological perspective shifted tremendously. initially, I just replaced the African American Baptist tradition with an E.T. overview. At the time, it may have appeared that in my theology, the Star People were Christian, although I most likely would not have said this at the time. Well, not exactly Christian, but all that had changed after my preliminary research was that Jesus was a Star Person; the rest of my theology remained the same.

Yet to even go this far, I had to overcome a tremendous amount of fear. I had to summon the courage to speak and write about this and mind you; there are a very few clergy members who agree with me; Dr. Barry Downing is one of them. He wrote a book called *U.F.O.s In The Bible,* which influenced me greatly. Yet Dr. Downing, to my knowledge, is not an Experiencer. The rabbit-hole went much deeper. I had to explore even further, which seems like what these intelligences wanted me to do in hindsight.

That is what life's journey is all about; asking questions, making decisions, and asking more questions, and living one's beliefs and principles. I began to see that Jesus was one of many great teachers whose teachings have influenced humankind but certainly not the only one. This argument made many people nervous because I was implying that Christianity was not as unique as some people of faith proclaimed it to be. In other words, it wasn't that the Christian story of the birth of Jesus and his life featured non-human intelligences in the story, but they were most likely a part of all of the stories of the bible and other sacred scriptures as well.

Secondly, if there was, in fact, a God or a Creator, it was not an anthropomorphic being with the same likes and dislikes as ordinary human beings. Still, perhaps it was best described as an Energy, an Intelligence, a "Universal Consciousness," "The Force", "Universal Mind" call it what you will. You see, the name doesn't really matter. I begin to get it that I was, that I am, and that I will always be a vital part of this energy and not separate from it, and most importantly---so is everyone and everything else is as well.

I recall how my fear kept me from going public with these thoughts and ideas for quite some time.

The spiritual journey that I was on was already beginning to shift a bit before my extraterrestrial contacts. I moved away from the more theologically conservative American Baptist tradition into an insatiable interest in comparative religious studies, especially those studies that focused on the mystical side of the various religious traditions.

I am reminded of the old bromide, "when the student is ready, the teacher will come." Yet after my first few contacts with the Visitors, this interest shifted even more deeply into meditation and prayer, spiritual metaphysics, reincarnation, spiritual healing, and psychic phenomena. In short, I was delving into what we used to call the occult, and the *study of human consciousness*. I began to focus on channeling and channeled material, palmistry, tarot and aura readings, as well as affirmative prayer and meditation.

My perspective shifted from an intellectual understanding of the interconnected oneness of all life on this planet to a more profound "inner knowing" that resonated with me on a deep level. I "felt" this connection in my body, mind, and spirit, realizing that what I do to another human being, another sentient or non-sentient being, or to the natural world, I was doing to myself. I began to crave and to spend more time in nature and near water. There was an inward journey, a journey without distance that I undertook that continues each day. Who am I beyond this flesh and personality? The word became flesh as I moved from an intellectual understanding of my life to living it and experiencing it daily. In short, my worldview was expanding.

The hidden anger that lurked beneath my behavior and personality that I held in my life gradually began to dissipate. I needed less and less to always have the answers and be right about things. I became less controlling, willing to risk being vulnerable, and became more authentic. Perhaps more human is another way of expressing this transformation. In short, what I had experienced was nothing short of a type of ego death, at least to the point that it was not always needing to the show. My relationships with others became more and more harmonious, especially the relationship with myself.

To be clear, there was a lot of hard work to peel back the layers and begin seeing myself with a bit more clarity. I had undergone seven years of Gestalt Therapy as well. Yet somehow, I felt that my spiritual learning was accelerated because of my contact experiences. Yes, I still had the challenges of living on this planet as a human being, but the scales were somehow removed from my eyes. I did not see the world with a jaundiced eye but with a new vision, a new clarity, and a renewed zest for life. I was more loving and forgiving in my outlook and actions.

That is not to say that I have become enlightened or that I am in some way superior to my fellow human beings. I am saying that I began to realize that I am much more powerful and accountable for my life than I had even started to imagine. I was beginning to grow up.

Along with this came a profound love and respect for the star people, my fellow human beings, and this planet. I began to love these non-human intelligences and to view them as simply my brothers and sisters. I still do, and I always will. My contacts still continue, sometimes with years in between.

Chapter Two

The Indicators

Any sufficiently advanced technology is indistinguishable from magic.
- Arthur C. Clark

I have been asked many times to counsel Experiencers. I assist them in finding ways to face, then work through their trauma. Eventually, if they do the work, they can place their experiences into context and move on with their lives. To be sure - *unresolved trauma will resurface!*

If you are an Experiencer or someone who may be an Experiencer, this book was written for you. No one likes to face their trauma. However, unless you meet it, the buried memories will continue to haunt you. Understanding the nature of the trauma and crisis experienced is the first step toward healing.

Some signs point out the possibility that you may be an Experiencer. There may be personality changes, a new awareness of the world around you, intense emotional states of being, and a renewed sense of the potential for change in yourself and the world around you. Below you will find possible clues or indicators that may be helpful.

Beliefs as Indicators

- Interest in UFOs. An idea that they exist.
- Faith in other dimensions and that intelligent life resides there.
- An interest in ancient history, metaphysics, and the occult sciences.
- A deep concern for and a feeling of urgency about the destruction of our ecosystem.
- Thoughts of impending earth and societal changes.
- Questioning the status quo.
- A motivation for equality and justice.
- A sense of being a citizen of the galaxy as opposed to a nationalistic perspective.
- A deep conviction against the fighting of wars.
- Visions of a united world.
- A thought, belief, or an idea that earth is not your true home.
- Knowing and believing there is more to life than what we are told.
- A decision to no longer support industrial food practices, which may entail eating only local or organically grown produce and meats, or a completely vegetarian or vegan diet/lifestyle.

Physical Indicators

- Dreams or nightmares of strange beings and other worlds.
- Dreams that are precognitive, inspirational, or that contain pertinent information.
- Dreams of meeting other beings, levitating, or flying.
- Dreams of healing or being healed, teaching or being taught.
- Skills in telepathy, clairaudience, clairvoyance, psychometry, or telekinesis.
- Periods of terror, anxiety for no apparent reason.
- Unexplained appearance of strange marks, scars, cuts, burns or bruises, particularly in the morning following a deep sleep or strange dreams.
- Memories that do not quite fit the facts of an activity, such as an event from early childhood.
- Unexplained aborted pregnancies.
- Hair and nails are growing faster than usual.
- Needing less sleep and having vast amounts of energy physically.
- Somehow feeling more "intelligent" or mentally having access to more information, downloading more wisdom and knowledge.
- Missing periods of time.
- Many Experiencers report nosebleeds, especially as children.

Spiritual Indicators

- Significant or sudden reversals in religious thoughts or feelings.
- An intense desire to study comparative religions.
- A desire or belief that humankind can attain a more advanced state of consciousness and a more evolved spirituality.
- An intense desire to serve humanity in some way, shape, or form.

If you believe or suspect that you are an Experiencer, then you have entered another world. That does not mean you are more special or gifted than those in the population who have not had the same experience. It does mean that you have begun an initiation, a journey, and how far you choose to travel is entirely up to you. The world of contact is a mysterious place, a place where you can become confused and lost. There is so much misinformation and disinformation out there.

Our personalities are built upon certain beliefs, values, and societal influences around ideas regarding what is "real." Consensus reality influences morality, religion, the obligation to self, family, and humanity. Trust in these structures and thoughts upholds the continuity of life. When traumatic or events of high strangeness occur, these ideas and systems are put to the test. Are they strong enough to sustain the impact of this other "reality?" The nature of the contact experience encompasses all areas of life and will test the boundaries of what is acceptable or considered real. The basic ideas or structures may not be able to withstand the impact of the contact experience.

You have an absolute right to address your contact experience in your own manner and time. It would be best if you discovered your path, your own truth. You can choose to identify as a victim, you can choose to deny your experience, or you can choose to integrate your experience into your life in a positive manner. No one can choose for you, so you must remember that whatever path you decide to take is your choice and responsibility.

It is easy to see when one researches the history of the UFO phenomena; there is almost always someone who will debunk, discredit, or discount the evidence presented by the experiencer. That has been going on since 1945 when UFOs became part of the national conversation in this country. Possibly this is true throughout history as well. I hope this book will assist you in remembering that you are not alone and that you and your experiences are significant and may assist humanity in creating a paradigm shift. You do not want to be a victim, nor are you a victim. Experiencers are taking their power back and becoming participants in this unfolding drama.

All cultures create norms for behavior within that society. Maybe none more so than ours, at this time. The people whose experiences or behavior does not fall within the range of those standards are not acknowledged, or worse, ostracized. Extraterrestrial contact or abduction does not fall within the norms of any modern society, although it does in some indigenous cultures. The challenge is to reconstruct societal views to expand and evolve the thinking and perceptions. This new reality can at least be seen as a genuine possibility if not accepted outright. Usually, these experiences, if taken to be credible, are thought of as unfavorable. Words such as "alleged," "abductee," "aliens," all have negative connotations, that imply victimization.

When you start to believe these labels, you are participating in your own victimization. It is still prevalent in society to blame the victim, blaming people because of their experiences. We see this commonly in rape cases, an assignment of victim status, a judgment, and a label imposed on one person by another. It is also a hallmark of ignorance and fear. Lack of belief by others is also a form of victimization and fear. When doubt is cast on a person as to their truthfulness, reliability, and mental stability, victimization may occur. The experiencer, without proper nonjudgmental support, can feel isolated, alone, shunned.

Most importantly, though, the goal is to understand yourself and discern how you can integrate the contact experience into your daily life. To be healed, you need to integrate the experience, not just survive it. You have to meet the challenges of the Star People as well as the challenges presented to you by humanity. You can do it!

I would be remiss in not acknowledging that although I eventually came to see my personal contact experiences as a gift, a gift that brought me profound growth and transformation, initially, I was terrified. As I mentioned in sharing my personal story, I sought a mental health professional and suffered from PTSD for many years. I would not trade these experiences for anything, yet it was a difficult path to tread in the beginning. I will share the checklist below for those still wrestling with what may or may not have happened to you. I have adapted it, with permission, from a book entitled *Healing Shattered Reality: Understanding Contactee Trauma,* by Alice Bryant and Linda Seebach.

Post-Contact Checklist

The following checklist is a quick reference to evaluate to what degree and how often Post Contact Experience occurs. Just note how often, prevalent and how many of these experiences you have. Of course, many of these things are within the range of the average person's experiences. But the sum of them, taken together, may indicate that you are an Experiencer and didn't know it - or an Experiencer and do know it but weren't sure if your behaviors or symptoms were due to that.

Often? Sometimes? Never?

- Anxiety or panic attacks
- Nightmares of Strange Beings with an other-worldly Flavor
- Sleep Avoidance/ or Irregular sleep patterns
- Early Morning Awakening
- Intense Vigilance
- Feelings of being watched
- Avoiding certain areas that make you uneasy.
- Anger out of context
- Unable to discuss UFO Experiences.
- Feelings of separation
- Frequent depression
- Constantly moving from place to place
- Problems sustaining intimate relationships.
- Keeping secrets
- Drinking and Drugging or other addictions
- Suicidal Thoughts
- Nosebleeds
- Intense reactions to stories, photos or films on the topic of UFOs or ETs.
- Unexplained marks on your body

Other clues may be nosebleeds, being very sensitive to pollutants, or suffering from allergies. Fear of the dark from childhood until adulthood is another clue. Do you have sudden premonitions and intuitive flashes? Are you constantly feeling watched or have visions of seeing the star's eyes, especially the Gray star beings?

That is not an exhaustive list, nor does it mean that other mental or emotional issues are undergirding the list above. It is a checklist for a *post-contact experience.* It is simply a self-analysis tool. You may use it to determine where you may need some assistance, and you may use it to become aware of certain behaviors. You may also use it to help you uncover areas in your life that may need scrutiny; by looking at what is happening *currently* and *in the past.*

Many Experiencers share these traits:

- Open-mindedness
- Curiosity or investigative nature
- Generosity
- Concern with global challenges and a willingness to help make the world a better place
- Wanting to serve humanity
- Courage
- Endurance & durability
- Lovingness and kindness

Do you recall at any time, or several times, making a declaration of intent to help humanity or expressing a desire to be of use in the world? That does not mean that everyone who has expressed this desire is an Experiencer, but Experiencers have these character traits in common.

You may understand that all initiation usually involves:

- Isolation or separation from others.
- Being led or sent sooner or later into a circular place or round enclosure.
- The assignment of teachers or mentors
- The assignment of disciplines or ordeals
- Spending a good deal of time learning traditions and spiritual purposes of a community or society.
- The acceptance of tasks with a sense of climbing higher or ascension while undertaking a journey.
- Attainment of powers or abilities
- Acceptance into a higher order or a place of greater responsibilities.

To my knowledge, all initiations follow this same pattern to a greater or lesser degree. That is especially evident in one of the most profound initiations known to human beings— the ordination of priests or ministers. This sort of initiation begins with the declaration of intent and separation for years of study. Vows will be made, teachers are provided, disciplines, tasks, and ordeals are undertaken, and a total commitment is finally made to a way of life. That is what you, as an Experiencer, are undergoing. Do you say you did not declare intent? Think again.

Chapter Three

The Separation

All truth comes in three stages. First, it is ridiculed. Second, it is violently opposed. Third, it is accepted as being self-evident.''
- Arthur Schopenhauer

Each Experiencer's experience is individual and unique, just we all are unique individuals. However, all initiations seem to follow the same basic rules or formula. The first step is to isolate the initiate, somehow cut them off from the herd, and separate them from their "community." The initial contact experience does this by its otherworldliness, then in friends and neighbors' reaction to the recounting of the event. They feel alone, isolated, and worried about the experience.

In ancient societies, the initiate, usually at puberty, is taken from the mother for a rite of passage. The youngster is removed from their family for a while, sometimes as long as a year or more. During this time, they are subject to personal hardships, over and beyond just being away from family and community. When the initiation is complete, the youngster returns to their family and the community as a full-fledged community member, ready to take on new and exciting responsibilities. Joseph Campbell, the great mythologist, describes that as an archetype of *The Hero's Journey.* It has been a recurring theme throughout history and cultures, dating back to the earliest recorded stories.

In a sense, that is your journey as an Experiencer, except you return to a larger worldwide community of humanity. That is your new role; to be a guidepost or beacon in the new world. Or maybe even an interplanetary, intergalactic cosmic community. We don't know how far our experiences will take us, but we are on the way.

The fact that no one might take your story seriously or even listen to it will further engender your feeling of separation. Maybe no one wants to deal with or even hear about the emotional uncertainties that may plague you. Suppose you have ongoing contact experiences, telepathy, night visions, or dreams that are too vivid to be ordinary dreams. In that case, you may even become dependent on your Star People, no matter how they present themselves. Relationship and family discord can quickly arise at this time.

That is the time to seek help and find someone or a group you trust and talk to them. It's what I had to do. It made my journey so much easier. Ironically, in today's culture, if you are something of an introvert, a loner, a free thinker, even a rebel, you may have it easier than most. If you are open to it, you may be guided, and you must trust that. The dreams you may have about a worldwide catastrophe are not meant to show you what is necessarily going to happen, but what could happen if humanity does not begin to wake up from this illusion that we are all separate from each other. We are shown the future *probabilities and possibilities,* not unalterable facts.

Remember, somewhere along the journey, you decided that you wanted to serve humanity, to assist your fellow human beings. Perhaps these experiences are part of the journey. Be prepared. Honest, mindful self-analysis is the key to spiritual growth. As for being alone, those who reject you are more afraid than you are. You are courageous, or you would not still be here. There are hundreds and thousands of other Experiencers out there, many of whom have never spoken up as yet. If you were indeed "crazy," would you work this hard to give others so much hope?

You are not alone. You are not crazy. The passage of time is now bringing the truth. Our government admits that we are witnessing UFOs in our skies (now commonly referred to by our military as *Unidentified Arial Phenomena).* Call it what you will. As Shakespeare reminds us in Romeo and Juliet, "What's *in a name?" That which we call a rose by any other name would still smell as sweet."* In other words, what matters is what something is, not what it is labeled.

Here is a list of questions to consider before and after your experience.

What was your belief and attitude concerning the following:

1. Ghosts
2. Life after death. Spirits of the deceased.
3. Reincarnation
4. Nature spirits
5. Gods and Goddesses of the mythologies
6. Satan and demons
7. God
8. Angels
9. Prophets
10. Messiahs
11. Purpose of your life
12. Purpose of humanity
13. Evolution
14. Astrology
15. Religion in general
16. Witches and Warlocks
17. Goblins, trolls, leprechauns

Did you or do you now believe in?

- Dreams and dream interpretation
- Talisman of good fortune
- Wearing of crystals or amulets

- Divine reward and punishment. Appeasement of the gods.
- Miracles and miraculous events
- Did you attend séances, spiritualist churches, gathering where psychic phenomena were displayed or studied?

Did you study these things seriously? Did you research alone or with others? Were you cautious or secretive about these studies and beliefs? Did you expect monetary reward or fame? Did you study hard? Were you patient or impatient in seeing results? Can you or were you able to deal with disappointment and still forge ahead? How do these questions make you feel? Do you think that you may have been chosen or have a mission to accomplish during this lifetime, contributing to raising the frequency on this planet from fear to love?

Do you habitually, sometimes, or never:

- Read science fiction?
- Study psychic or occult literature?
- Watch space movies or space programs on TV?
- Peruse UFO Literature

Do you:

- Anticipate Doomsday Prophecies?
- Worry about the fate of humanity?

· Life after death?

Are you looking for assistance from:

· Divine intervention
· Religious or spiritual philosophies
· Governmental intervention?
· Science, technology, education?
· Extraterrestrials?
· As time went on after your initial contact experience, did you find yourself drifting away from former associates and spending more time alone?
· Do you feel you have a part to play in coming events?
· If you had the opportunity to perform some task, large or small, to make the world a healthier, happier place, would you do it?

Those items may offer a clue as to why you may have been contacted. No, this is not a definitive answer, yet those individuals that are experiencers and view the experience ultimately as something positive and transformational have these items in common.

According to Mark Rodeghier, Scientific Director of UFO Studies, there is a selection of criteria for "Abductees."

A Person Must Be Taken:

- Against their own will.
- From Terrestrial Surroundings
- By Non-human Beings

The Beings Must take The Person To:

- An Enclosed Place
- Not Terrestrial in Appearance
- Assumed or known to be a spacecraft by a witness

In This Place the Person Must Either:

- Be subjected to an examination
- Engage in Communication (Verbal or Telepathic)
- Or both

These Experiences May Be Remembered:

- Consciously
- Or Through Methods of Focused Concentration (E.g., Hypnosis)

Notice that this definition excludes people who have what is known as a bedroom experience, "where a person recalls some activities of beings or other unusual phenomena in the bedroom but doesn't have any knowledge or memory of physically leaving the bedroom." I fall into this category, yet under hypnosis, I was removed from my bedroom.

It also excludes people who may have had their contact experience out of doors but let's further explore. The enclosure may also be a round or oval room, a craft, or even a round field, a ballpark, even a car could fit the description well enough. Does it always have to be against an individual's will? Can one be led to this place consciously or unconsciously?

The circle or round enclosure can symbolically represent new beginnings for the initiate. It can be a vision quest of sorts, like emerging from the womb, a rebirth. In ancient times, the enclosure could have been a hut or even a cave or a sweat lodge, yet the idea is the same. When you emerge again from your surroundings, you are not the same person as before. You are "reborn," and you have begun a transformation.

When you had your initial contact experience, were you in a car, an open field, a circular place? If taken aboard a craft, what was the shape of the room? How long after the event did you have a recall? Did your recall come naturally, or was hypnosis involved? Did you have memory trouble, and was time distorted in any way for you?

Chapter Four

The Teachers and Mentors

The discovery of life beyond earth would trans-form not only our science but also our religions, our belief systems, and our entire worldview. For in a sense, the search for extraterrestrial life is really a search for ourselves---who we are and what our place is in the grand sweep of the cosmos.
- Paul Davies, The Harmony of The Spheres

Now we arrived at the stage, also found in Joseph Campbell's work on "The Heroes Journey," where you, the hero, or shero, have accepted the call and will now get to meet a mentor or mentors to encourage you to pursue your journey with confidence. Anyone wise and experienced can assist you in the journey as you face yourself and your uncertainties. The teacher(s) or mentor(s) can be a group of individuals or a single person. I have found that it will usually be all of the above. At the beginning of my journey after the initial experience, I sought out a therapist who assisted me in holding on to my sanity. I also found a group of like-minded Experiencers, and so I became part of a community. These teachers were vital to my transformation and affirming my experience as one of learning to accept myself, others, and the ability to love.

It is also important to note that our teachers and mentors may not always be people we like. They can even be seen as enemies. They may not always be what we consider as humans. However, they will place a mirror up to us to see ourselves, warts, and all on the journey to acceptance. These teachers are just as important as the ones we embrace and enjoy being around. That is important to remember as we embark on our journey.

Here is a list of what Experiencers may expect on the journey with their tutor or mentor:

- Some form of "baptism." A life-changing experience.
- The appearance of a tutor, a mentor, a guide or instructor, perhaps several initially, but eventually settling down to one.
- Participation in disciplines, vows, rituals, fasts, vigils, journeys or quests.
- Some journeys may be more of an inner journey than traveling from location to location.
- Learning of traditions, ancient religions or lan-

guages, myths, and symbols. Ancient civilizations such as Sumer, Egypt, Peru, Mayan, U.S. Native American, and other aboriginal cultures.

· Receiving revelations or secrets.
· Sometimes the development of innate talents or abilities is necessary, taking up a creative work abandoned in the past.
· Gaining more self-confidence, more focus, or direction in one's daily living.

Now, a word about intimate relationships for those of us who are Experiencers.

Intimate Relationships and The Experiencer

Relationships, even the most emotionally healthy relationships, take commitment and self-awareness. For those of us who are Experiencers, these relationships can be incredibly challenging. I have been fortunate enough in my relationship history to have had understanding partners, even when they did not always understand what I was going through when dealing with my contact experiences. Not everyone can be so fortunate. Yet we must remember that our partners can be our teachers and mentors as well, whether we like it or not.

One of the enhancements of the contact experience is to see the world in a different light. Even when you have your own emotions under control and feel steady on your inner foundations--- friends, family, partners, and or spouses seem to have changed. But they have not changed---you have. You find yourself in situations where it is possible to learn and grow, yet at times, you may remain in a particular set of circumstances even after that learning is complete.

Patience is key. If you become impatient and retreat from a situation or relationship before your lessons are learned, it will reappear in your life again somewhere down the road. That can happen more often than is spoken about as the Experiencer may begin to feel that they have somehow "outgrown" the relationship. That is most obvious in second and third marriages where the new spouse is in some ways a carbon copy of the former one. However, the physical appearances may vary significantly. Many Experiencers become restless and may want to move on with relationships left unresolved. That is not always necessary or wise.

In a perfect world, committed intimate partners (married or otherwise) share in their spiritual development. One of the most difficult is when one partner or spouse, often due to the experience itself, begins the psychic and spiritual development path, and the other partner simply cannot or will not join in. It happens. That puts tremendous stress on the relationship.

There is a point of no return in developing the awareness of the "Higher Self" and to the commitment to the direction you feel you may be headed. Once reached, it is challenging to resume former attitudes. You are responsible for your own soul's development. You may experience a betrayal of self and turn away from your path of evolvement due to pressure caused by the insecurities and the divergent realities of your loved ones. Not many marriages or other committed relationships can stand the strain of this type of tension. If the connection is to be healed, it must occur in the beginning stages when a compromise can be reached. It is also important to note that the ending of a relationship is not always a sign of failure. Sometimes lessons are learned, and it is time to move on. Again, impatience can be detrimental to the partnership.

Many Experiencers soon feel they no longer fit their old patterns. They are like square pegs in a round hole. The holes must be enlarged for the old fit will never work again. To inform you, the divorce rate for Experiencers is high. Spouses and significant others of Experiencers undergo a particular type of trauma uniquely their own. First and foremost is the feeling of being left out, of missing an event that has made a tremendous impression on the husband, wife, or partner. Dealing with the resultant emotional stress and the almost inevitable personality changes—both positive and negative—takes a great deal of maturity, openness, and discernment.

If the person who is not an Experiencer does not believe in the phenomena, issues of credibility arise. The non-Experiencer may resort to ridicule, scorn, or derision. They may even make fun of the Experiencer out of a sense of uneasiness or downright fear.

Fear of the unknown can take many forms. The Experiencer, suffering from their own fears and phobias, may refuse to communicate, thus further stressing the relationship.

Spouses or partners of Experiencers sometimes complain of feeling shut out, which is quite likely a legitimate complaint. That is especially true if the Experiencer has found a support system outside of their family. There is a tendency for those who have had the contact experience to establish strong bonds and connections with others who have also had an experience, eventually widening the family communication gap.

If the event is made public, the spouse or partner is inadvertently caught up in the public eye, willingly or not, and may suffer ego-threatening exposure having to answer questions about an event that they may or may not perceive as reality. Some spouses or partners long to have an experience of their own and worry about why it does not happen to them. They may feel inadequate, secretly unworthy, envious, and even jealous. These are all emotions that can be difficult to handle if you don't already have good communication habits within the relationship.

A sense of boredom may eventually set in. The partner cannot share in the adrenalin rush of excitement generated by the experience. It isn't easy to generate enthusiasm for an event they may not perceive as real. If the Experiencer is in denial, the nightmares, restless need to move from place to place, and the possibility of the Experiencers dependency on substances such as alcohol or drugs to cope can be hard for the partner or spouse to accept. The Experiencer may become moody or indifferent out of the sheer frustration from the feelings of helplessness.

Experiencers tend to change life goals, interests, and often careers. That can be extremely difficult for a spouse or partner who may see no reason for such major life changes or adjustments. Spouses or partners may be deeply distressed when longing to put down roots when faced with a transient lifestyle caused by the Experiencer's constant need to be on the move. Understanding the underlying cause will enable the spouse or partner to comprehend the Experiencer's need to be on the move and help the Experiencer address the issues behind that need.

Spouses or partners are as much in need of support as the Experiencer. There is a need to develop empathy for each other's feelings. Empathy is more important than sympathy because empathy is indicative of a more harmonious relationship. The important thing here is how the situation is being handled. Communication, patience, understanding, and openness are necessary for both individuals' mental health and well-being. Here, professional couples or family therapy may be of help.

The Experiencer needs to share their profound emotional experiences, especially the fears. Both must seek to educate themselves to understand better that they are not alone and that many others are undergoing the same stresses. Understanding the phenomenon (as much as humanly possible) enables partners to cope with the high strangeness, the sheer bizarreness of these experiences in a better way. The understanding gained through education will assist in reducing the fear factor.

Chapter Five

The Trials, Disciplines and Vows

Do not be conformed to this world, but be transformed by the renewing of your mind.
- Romans 12:2

Ridicule is one of the ordeals through which the initiate must pass. It is one of the most cutting and can inflict severe emotional pain. The challenge is to make peace with yourself and your experience. You know it is the truth. In what way it was the truth we may not know. But maybe you can find a reason for the experience, and by finding a basis, come to some peace within yourself. That will permit you to endure and look with some understanding upon those who ridicule us. For you see, they are afraid; just as fearful as we are. Those who have not experienced it cannot know. They mock us mainly from the fear of examining the unknown too closely. Fear, envy, and perhaps other factors prompt the ridicule-you did not create it.

Perhaps you may hold your head in your hands and wonder, "Why me?", they are asking themselves, "Why not me?" "Why have you been favored with this experience and not they?" Disciplines are taken on. The first crucial one is to learn to forgive yourself for the mistakes and errors of the past. All spiritual disciplines require this to move forward. You may find yourself picking over the events of your life and re-living painful memories, examining and re-examining them. A kind of mental catharsis takes place, relieving you of the condemnation and profound regret over events you felt should have been handled better. You come to see that you are not a bad person.

This catharsis may take years, but it is the first and necessary step to bring the pattern of belief into a workable arrangement for the life to be led. The second step is the opportunity to learn, to extend your knowledge of many things, people, and places. To fill in your educational gaps, not necessarily by going to school but by travel, new experiences, exposure to new ideas, and contact with diverse people. Old ideas and ways of looking at things will be shed, with a tentative trying on of the new. If there is resistance to change, the journey will become more arduous, and you may become stunted in your growth.

Mysteries will begin to make sense or "add up" only when you have reached a certain level of understanding and sophistication. These may resemble clues to a detective story, and only much later will their purpose, use, value, and meaning be understood. An example of these "mysteries" need not always be grandiose. Let's say a particular type of book needs to be read. The right person comes along and recommends it to you, or it is sent as a gift. Perhaps you feel the need to peruse certain books that you become "inspired" to read. Or you meet the right person at the right time in your life, and they may have information or knowledge that you need at that particular time. There is a certain effortless flow and synchronicity to your life as you walk your path. That signifies that you are moving in the right direction. It isn't all about actions taken; you may even find yourself *not* doing something you had planned.

There comes a time after you have forgiven yourself for all of your supposed wrongdoings or "sins" and you begin to reevaluate your beliefs. Now you start to work on your dependence on others. Perhaps, that is especially challenging for life has taught you more about your weaknesses than your strengths. You may be tempted to lean heavily or lightly on the shoulder, or the strong back of some authority figure, to whom you give allegiance, and all too often, your strength.

Difficult circumstances may arise, and they may make your task a weary one. Yet, the circumstances or events will reveal you to yourself and make you aware of who you are, and also who you can become.

Box: 1 of 1

Tracking#: 278081567412

Total Items: 1

Always the choice is yours. Believing in yourself, you have matured into a person that is now ready for your mission. There is something to be aware of, and that is the human tendency to entertain the unhealthy ego behaviors we all present. The task is not to debate whether the human ego must be battled and defeated or allowed to run free.

The wise would say that a healthy ego is the goal and not to do away with something useful and inherent in everyone. Awareness, here, is critical; the ego does not have to rule. Mediation is one path to becoming aware of the movement of your mind and ego- and with this awareness; you begin to have a choice in how you think. If you continue to observe your thoughts without judgment, you are on the way to developing discernment. This quality is necessary for your journey.

Those Experiencers who elevate themselves without valid reason and find themselves unable to come down from their lofty towers of ego proclaim, "I am special," "I am gifted," because of my experiences, *and you are not*, will fall. Those Experiencers who babble on and on about past experiences, not advancing one step further in the direction of human evolution or collaborating with the cosmic forces and principles that guide them are simply not aware of the movement of their minds. Indeed, such persons may give a bad reputation to the entire realm of UFO-Contact Experiences. On the other hand, we each can only work within our capacity at any given time. Try not to be overly judgmental of others; work on yourself. It helps to remember the wise observation that those who most annoy us are reflecting our own shadow side back to us.

There remains one further step now. Eventually, you will become free of all that would hinder you in your journey to your destiny. You must not abandon your task for the sake of clinging demands from others. It would be best to become wise and patient to consider and reconsider what is necessary and advantageous to your path and who and what is hindering, confining, or obscuring. Some of your most cherished and basic beliefs may need to be re-examined from the view of this "new" self. You may need to loosen some of your strongest ties.

That does not mean abandoning family, friends, or social responsibilities. It means careful measuring of time, energy and talents, to give each its just and honorable due, but no more. No sacrificing of one to the other; simply a re-prioritizing of your time and energy. That is the most challenging assignment of all, but it must be done because, after all, in the long run, it is the path that you chose for yourself.

Have you ever been instructed or felt compelled to:

- Diet or to change your diet?
- Observe better health habits?
- Organize your time better?

- Be more practical with money?
- Restructure your fundamental beliefs?
- Led to study certain things? Lucid Dreaming, Out of Body Experiences?
- Do you recall making any formal vows?
- As a result of your "experiences" are you now more self-dependent, more self-assured, have more self-esteem?

Chapter Six

Cultural Traditions and Research

Almost all initiates study the spiritual traditions of their own people, but the Experiencer explores cultural traditions from around the globe. Learning traditions means studying the following:

- Creation Stories Of How The Earth Came To Be.
- The Creation of Humanity.
- The Primal Cause of this Creation.
- Heroes and Sheroes of Old.
- Ancient Ones Who Formulated Moral Codes and Social Laws.
- Sky Gods
- Relationships Between Human Beings and The Animal Kingdom.
- Relationships Between Human Beings and Nature.

Many Experiencers, after contact, find themselves traveling to places of archaeological and anthropological significance to study and research. Peoples such as the Sumerians, Babylonians, Akkadians, Assyrians, ancient Egypt, Incas, Mayans, Aztecs, and Native American cultures are good to research. You will find that all of these cultures have stories of "Sky Gods" interacting with their population. Another area of study for those who are not interested in the studies of ancient civilizations might be the study of comparative religions. The sacred scriptures: the Vedas of India, the Popol Vuh of The Mayans, the Egyptian or Tibetan Book of The Dead, as well as the writings of the Bible and The Quran, may hold your interest as well.

After my initial experiences, I studied all of the above, and my thirst for this knowledge proved almost insatiable. It helped me realize that these cultures had plenty of contact with off-world intelligences. They were given laws and wisdom regarding how to live with each other and the natural world, laws that we still find difficult to follow in order to share this planet peaceably with each other. Perhaps the study of ancient languages and symbols is where your interests may lie. Some Experiencers have been given alphabets and vocabularies in what are purported to be languages from other planets.

Or you may feel the need to travel, visit other cultures, and interact with people who are different from you. You may not even know why you want to travel, and that's perfectly fine as what you need to be revealed will eventually become clear. It will help if you trust this. My first contact experience occurred after returning from visiting the Mayan pyramids on the Yucatan Peninsula. Years later, I visited Jerusalem and some of the sacred sites in that part of the world, years before it even occurred to me to write my books on UFOs and The Bible. Both of those trips prepared me for the books long before I had even thought of writing them. Coincidence? Maybe. But Albert Einstein reminds us that "God does not play dice."

- Have you ever felt compelled to go to certain places for research or study? If so, where and for what purpose?
- Have you been led to study world religions? If so, which ones?
- Have you been led to study metaphysical subjects?
- Have you spent much time studying mythologies? Which ones?
- Have you felt a connection with studying Native American culture? Other aboriginal peoples?
- Have you felt compelled to study psychic phenomena?
- What do you feel you have learned from these studies?

Tasks or Assignments

Experiencers are men and women existing in places worldwide like China, Sweden, Brazil, Australia, Africa, Europe, and the United States. The tasks that they are assigned are in total harmony with their own particular time and place. The insistence that Experiencers study the cultures and religions of ancient civilizations and one's own is not to make any one culture superior. Instead, it shows us the diversity and often the similarities among these cultures, moves us out of the narrow and provincial spheres where we sometimes dwell and into a worldwide, deep comprehension of the ways and thoughts of humanity as a whole.

At times, these tasks may feel like climbing a ladder, a ladder to a new world that you are about to enter. You realize that the world may not have to change so much as your idea about the world had to change. One begins to "see the light." Things that have happened to you start to make sense. You begin to understand meanings and purposes and see why certain things occurred when they occurred and that they had to occur in the way they did. This new world we are entering seems overly technological but is undergirded by a deep and abiding spirituality, for if it is not, we as human beings will destroy ourselves. That has indeed been the message from some "star races" to humanity. Our technological prowess has outdistanced our humanity.

Some Experiencers will find their tasks in creative endeavors, such as writing, drawing, painting, photography, or in areas of scientific research. Other tasks will indeed be in technological advancement, but to use this technology, not for the manufacturing of weapons systems but for the better of humankind. Our institutions, financial, social, educational, and religious, will feel the impact and the necessity for change. Experiencers will be the driving force behind this new consciousness. It is a time when the lapses and misdirections of the current institutions will bring an inner collapse, brought on by their resistance to change.

Our institutions cannot continue with this old way of functioning and flourish in the new age to come. New ways of being and thinking, choosing cooperation over the competition by governments and the human community will nullify the old way of thinking and being. It is happening now in our lifetimes. Technologically speaking, as more and more sophisticated communication devices multiply and become available and spread globally, secrets and secrets operations become less and less possible.

The tasks that Experiencers are given are to contribute to a world where cooperation matters. It seems we are to assist in creating a world where human beings go above and beyond their view of the world as made up of elite politicians and armies' policies and nation-states. This new possibility of living as "citizens of the world" is an authentic goal to be worked toward and realized.

There are indeed other tasks that Experiencers may be compelled to pursue, which is the task of developing their psychic abilities. Many Experiencers have noted that after their contact experiences, they have an increase in these abilities. Some Experiencers go into psychic healing or bodywork. Some become mediums or channelers, practice automatic writing, while others go into the field of psychic research. Some develop the practice of intentional out-of-body experiences, remote viewing, lucid dreaming, telepathy, and heightened intuition. Discernment must also be developed along with those abilities.

The meaning of these abilities and the meaning of the contact experience are complex and complicated. There is much more than a single purpose going on. Each Experience is enormously complex, representing many levels or facets of meaning, various conditions of reality, and accomplishing an entire multitude of ends, all of this underlying the event itself. There is no single interpretation of any one event, just as there are differences between the beneficial and the mischievous psychic existences, so there are differences in psychic abilities. Just make sure you do not fall into the trap of thinking that spiritual gifts and psychic gifts are the same things and that they somehow make you special. Everyone has the capacity for them.

- Do you feel there is some larger task that you are being led to pursue, such as the study of ancient civilizations or religions?
- Do you believe that you have developed or are

developing psychic abilities as a result of your contact experiences?

- What was your introduction to the field of psychic phenomenon as a result of your contact experiences?
- Are you drawn to the healing arts? Massage, reflexology, energy healing such as Reiki, therapeutic touch, etc. Do you perceive energy emanating from your hands, or do you see colors or auras around people?
- Are you aware of past lives either as a human being or as a Star Being?
- Do you notice any difficulty or unusual occurrences around electronic devices?
- Do you experience feeling as if you cannot move at times while in bed or what is commonly referred to as sleep paralysis?

Chapter Seven

The Children

Are you experienced? Ah! Have you ever been experienced? Well, I have.
- Jimi Hendrix

Many children and adolescents are Experiencers. That I know from first-hand experience. Some of the characteristics named earlier in this book can be guideposts for learning if your child, or a child you know, may have had contact experiences with off-world intelligences or Star People. These children may also be known as Star Kids, or Indigo Kids, or Indigo Children.

Perhaps you had noticed that some children and teenagers today seem much more mature and more sensitive to their inner and outer worlds than we were growing up. I know that as a parent, I see this in my teenage daughter and her friends. Clearly, I am not saying that all the youngsters displaying some of the characteristics that I will detail are having off-world contacts. But there is the *possibility* that this may be happening. As parents and adults, we need to listen to them and what they may be trying to tell us.

Two very respected researchers that I know of who have done excellent work in the Star Children's field are Mary Rodwell and Dr. Richard Boylan. Mary is a trained hypnotherapist, mother, former nurse, and midwife. She was born in the UK and now resides in Australia. She is the author of the book, *Awakening: How Extraterrestrial Contact Can Transform Your Life.* Dr. Richard Boylan is a psychologist and clinical hypnotherapist who resides in Northern California. Dr.Boylan is the author of numerous books. One of those books is entitled *Star Kids: The Emerging Cosmic Generation.*

Mary Rodwell notes that these kids have an extremely high intelligence quotient and an intense commitment regarding the stewardship of the earth. Both authors report on the psychic ability of these youngsters and their recall of past lives on this, and other planets.

Rodwell lists some of the indicators which may be clues as to who may be a star child.

Here are a few indicators:

- Claim to feel different from parents or siblings
- Feel a sense of mission or purpose
- Feel very connected to all living things
- Drawing unusual pictures, symbols, scripts
- Feeling watched or observed

- Feel they are visiting other planets, existence, or realities
- Feel that they have been touched when resting or sleeping by something that could be described as non-human
- Feel that their body is too heavy or bulky.

Mary Rodwell believes that these children will grow up to populate the earth with "new human beings." Human beings that are more connected to the earth and their own cosmic heritage use their abilities and gifts to better the planet and a brighter future for all concerned.

Dr. Boylan has added other indicators. Again, this is not an exhaustive list.

- The child knows something intuitively about a person, a place, or a situation that turns out to be correct. The child is psychic.
- The child affects certain electrical appliances repeatedly by their presence.
- The child can see auras around other people or animals.
- The child may report visitations by Star People.
- The child's parents have had visits by Star People.
- The child exercises unusual adult-like initiatives for the social good.
- The child reacts with an unusually intense pos-

itive recognition or emotion to realistic photos or drawings of Star Visitors in magazines, television, or movies.

These children need to be nurtured as much as other children, but also need adults that support their unique perspectives and provide them with solid information and resources to satisfy their curiosity. They may be marginalized in school and lacking peer support. An attentive parent can help provide them with social options so that they may find like-minded peers, as well as allowing them to be introverted when they need to be. The key is helping them to find balance.

Chapter Eight

Wrapping it Up

The human failing I would most like to correct is aggression. It may have had a survival advantage in caveman days, to get more food, territory, or partner with whom to reproduce, but now it threatens to destroy us all.
-Stephen Hawking

In some ways, the final act of the initiatory process is to find a greater sense of freedom and a greater sense of responsibility. I am not saying here that your contact experiences are over, yet that may be the case. Depending on your particular type of experience, you may already begin to feel or sense this type of freedom and responsibility. For you see, there is so much that we don't know about the Star People and these experiences. My personal experiences were very loving, but we know that for many people, that has not been the case.

Many Experiencers have had life-long contacts and have developed close relationships with these beings.

That is not the case with all Experiencers. We know that the Star Beings gift some Experiencers with healing from illnesses and emotional trauma. That has not been the case with everyone. Why is that? The truth is we really don't know, at least not yet.

We know that there is a life transformation for those who have begun to see their experiences in a more positive light. I realize that this is not possible for many simply because the contact experience was not pleasant in the least. There is no way to see good happening from it until one deals with the trauma. Even then, it may not happen, depending on the contact experience itself. I am not suggesting that anyone sugarcoat their feeling regarding what happened to them. It doesn't do you any good to either deny trauma or let it define you.

Yet, we do know that contact Experiencers usually seek a universal spirituality, a more metaphysical view of life and the world in which we live. We understand that experiences with Star People often bring a new understanding of humanity's place in the cosmic scheme of things. As science begins to reveal objective truths regarding knowledge previously thought of as magic, occult, supernatural or superstitious, the Experiencer has more support and solid ground to explore.

The challenge remains to find your place in the immediate environment if you can or changing the situation. It can mean looking for productive relationships with your fellow human beings as well as with other

Experiencers. It can mean re-adjusting your life direction and intent, strengthening your will or motivation, re-assigning hours to more productive ends, gaining in self-confidence and courage, re-affirming faith in some greater power or plan or purpose.

Unfortunately, at least for now, the Experiencer will not receive much or any support from organized or even disorganized religion. On social change issues, be it race, gender equality, or even acknowledging the validity of other ways of worshiping, the contact experience presents a particular problem for some religions, especially the three "monotheistic faiths." I am speaking of Christianity, Judaism, and Islam. As a clergy person, it gives me no great joy to write this.

In my first book, *Alien Scriptures: Extraterrestrials in The Holy Bible,* I explained that I see these three faiths as originating from the contact experiences of human beings and that consciously or not, the Star People may have been the originators of the three monotheistic religions. To my mind, this in no way invalidates the beautiful and profound truths of these faith traditions. Yet, for many, my attempt to explain the stories of these faith traditions from a new and exciting perspective is nothing short of blasphemy and heresy. For instance, I have found that there is little room in the Judeo-Christian tradition for a variety of celestial beings who can cause a great deal of terror when they initially appear and bring with them an odd mixture of transcendence as well. They have no regard for religious dogma or hierarchy. To many religious leaders, this is highly threatening. It is one thing to say that we are not alone and that there is an over-riding *spirit* that is all around us and within us. It is quite another thing to have that "spirit" show up in our bedrooms, on long dusty rural roads while driving, or in our modern cities. Not to mention that these "spirits" are created in our image, at least partially.

That isn't easy to incorporate into our religious sensibilities, especially with the recent rise in Fun-damentalism in religions throughout the world. One common factor that all Fundamentalists share is in-tolerance. For many religious people, regardless of whether or not they have had a contact experience, these beings are the epitome of evil, disciples of the devil. It appears that the Eastern philosophies and re-ligions may be able to make room for them, if they have not already, mainly because of the non-dualism in which they view the cosmos.

The western mind and religious sensibilities to date still offer powerful resistance to acceptance. That may eventually change, but that change may be a while in coming. I remain hopeful as I have met a few clergy members in my travels who are open to this idea of rethinking the scriptures from an *Ancient Alien* perspective. Perhaps now that our government is becoming a bit more transparent regarding what they now term as UAP (Unidentified Aerial Phenom-ena) in our skies, maybe the religious establishment will not be far behind. Time will tell.

Now:

- Where do you feel you are in your process of initiation?
- Do you feel that your life has been improved by your contact experiences?
- Do you feel committed to the task, mission, or duty to prepare the world for the UFO message?
- Do you feel more powerful and supported in a way where you can be of service to others?

Think about these questions in the days, weeks, and months ahead; your answers will be the catalyst from which all of your actions grow.

I would be remiss if I did not mention a word to the researchers, who ideally will be working with the Experiencer as this new world and new consciousness is taking shape. The process, no doubt, is difficult for both parties because of the high strangeness of the event. That is even more of a challenge when the researcher has not had the experience themselves.

I am not a psychotherapist (I am a pastoral counselor) and do not pretend to be. Yet, I am an Experiencer which is why I feel qualified to write this guidebook. I do not pretend to have all of the answers.

I have discovered the following:

- Many Experiencers develop specific symptoms associated with significant trauma and may become dysfunctional due to that contact experience.

- The treatment of Experiencers as ordinary people who experienced deep trauma as opposed to psychotics or neurotics is crucial to healing.
- The researcher must expand understanding of the nature of reality and the effects of the contact experience upon that reality.
- The researcher must begin the cessation of victimization of Experiencers by the culture in which we live.

So this is it. I acknowledge that none of this makes sense to the Western scientific worldview. I often wonder what it will take to make the shift, but the transition will eventually happen. As discussed in previous chapters, a kind of cultural ego death is required. The Copernican revolution has shown us that the earth is not the center of the cosmos, which means that neither are we human beings. We are not the preeminent intelligent life in the multiverse. Experiencers remind us of this by their very existence.

We let people know that there are intelligent beings in the cosmos that are far more advanced than we are in certain aspects, and if they wanted to harm us, they would have done so by now.

Each Experiencer is on a journey like a pioneer. As they embark on the journey to process, then integrate their experience, and then relate it to the rest of the world, their consciousness opens to the existence of unknown dimensions of reality and the human psyche. I do not believe that Star Beings wish us ill. I think they are warning us that we are on the verge of destroying ourselves, as any good neighbor would.

Perhaps if we could just let go of the illusion of control and the need to be the masters of our world, we might discover our place as one species among many and that we are all connected in ways that we have yet to comprehend. I believe the connecting principle, the force that expands our consciousness beyond our little lives and selfish aims, is love. In your discovery of a loving interconnectedness, we might reach the tipping point. I believe it is our destiny to overcome our blindness, our idea of separateness, then evolve toward wholeness in the community of life. The earth will thank us for this new consciousness.

We have all read about or heard about the horror stories that have occurred to some Experiencers. As Experiencers, we may have had panic attacks. We may have sought answers in all of the wrong places and in places where no answers seemed to exist. Through our personal experience, we have developed certain beliefs. There are more questions than answers. Yet as researchers and Experiencers, we hope to shed some light, open some doors of awareness, give each other support and the space to find what rings true for us. I hope this book will provide you with cues and clues on your journey. The journey need not be burdensome. May you soon find your peace and your footing;

so that you may incorporate your experiences into a balanced life of service to the collective good of the planet, the multiverse, and all beings.

This is the new millennium; we have entered The Age of Aquarius. It can be an exciting and frightening time. It is clear to me that no savior is coming for us. Indeed, we are the ones we have been waiting for. The choice is up to each one of us.

PART TWO:
Transformation

Chapter Nine

The Spiritual
Transformation

Strange things are going on in ufology. They are fascinating partly because of their theological implications and partly because of the peculiar reaction of scientists...the scientist has scaled the mountains of ignorance; he is about to conquer the highest peak; as he pulls himself over the final rock, he is greeted by a band of theologians who have been sitting there for centuries.
- Dr. Robert Jastrow (*God and The Astronomers*)

In Part Two we will explore the Spiritual Transformation of UFO-related contact Experiencers as reflected in the F.R.E.E. Experiencer Research Study and from the Experiencer, Spiritual, and Consciousness literature. I will also share the words of five Experiencers.

FREE is the Dr. Edgar Mitchell Foundation for Research into Extraterrestrial Encounters. It is the first comprehensive research study on individuals that have had contact experiences with an unidentified flying object (UFO) and associated non-human intelligence (NHI). More specifically, this study represents the analysis of a large population that is both multi-language and cross-cultural.

Before going any further, I want to define the terms we are using. Please remember that words can sometimes get in the way, but words are all we have. The word *spiritual* means many things to many people. In this context, the word *spiritual* is a way to describe the individual who has been or is cultivating their inner life. In other words, an individual is navigating and excavating their sense of inherent worth and dignity. That intrinsic worth, grace, and moral compass guide their day-to-day existence. It is the mindful cultivation of one's inner life.

That is sometimes referred to as the inward journey, the existential journey, or the journey without distance. Many people are discovering, perhaps for the very first time, their individual and unique essence. This discovery may include questioning who they are, what they believe and why, their own moral and ethical standards. It provides an exploration of what it means to love and be loved in return and what it means to be in a relationship with others and oneself. Then, they can decide what this discovery will look like as they travel on their particular life path.

The journey of self-discovery affects their interactions with others and the entire planet.

It is not necessarily a religious journey, for there are times when religion can impede because it tends to reduce all of the mysteries of life into a formula with its focus on creeds and doctrines. Yet religion can play a major part in this inner excavation, exploration, and navigation; the spiritual journey may even transcend the religious one in many instances.

Transformation is another interesting word. Transformation implies a change of some sort, but I am referring to behavioral changes in one's perspective of reality in this context. In other words, an individual must sincerely want to change. This decision is crucial because, without intentionality, authentic transformation cannot occur. We cannot change or transform anyone else, but we can transform ourselves, and there may be certain circumstances or events that trigger this transformation. The circumstances that trigger an inner transformation can take place in a variety of ways. The following list is not exhaustive.

- The death of a loved one.
- A divorce or the breakup of a long-term relationship.
- A life-threatening illness for you or a loved one.
- Witnessing an event that is usually labeled impossible by the dominant culture or the culture one is born into because it defies the so-called societal norms.

Living is always an adventure, for life in its infinite wisdom appears to know just what slings and arrows of outrageous fortune are needed to get our attention, to wake us up. Events may not need to be as dramatic as the ones listed above. Human beings can learn from joy as well as pain. Certainly, watching a sunset or sunrise can affect us profoundly. Admiring or witnessing a beautiful work of art may do the trick. Gazing into a lover's eyes can also resonate with us on a deep level to effect lasting change. A hike in the forest or just spending time in nature may allow us to connect with that sense of something greater than ourselves. Yet we often seem to require something a bit more dramatic before we wake up to the unity, the preciousness, and the mystery that is life. I am no exception.

This section is about those individuals who have had contact with non-human intelligences and have acknowledged these contact as a positive and transformative experience. That is not to deny the experience of those brothers and sisters who have suffered the trauma of contact with less benevolent or evolved beings for whatever reason. After all, just because an individual or a civilization is more developed technologically does not mean they are more evolved morally, ethically, or spiritually. Just look at us!

In 1994, Dr. Richard Boylan, Ph.D., wrote a truly excellent book entitled, *Close Extraterrestrial Encounters: Positive Experiences with Mysterious Visitors*. In the book, he summarizes people who have had contact experiences when doing his research for this book. Dr. Boylan comes to the conclusions below.

After their experiences, one group:

· Sees the Star People as a threat, and they felt a great deal of powerlessness during and after the experience. In other words, they suffered from severe trauma.

The other group displayed the following characteristics:

· Curiosity about Star People
· Fascination with Star People contact
· Broadened Cosmic Perspective
· Global humanitarian concern
· Earth Ecology focus
· Friendly feelings towards Star People
· Tolerance for sharing the Earth
· Decreased materialistic focus.

Pulitzer Prize-winning author, Harvard professor, and UFO researcher, John E. Mack, M.D., also came to similar conclusions in his research into human transformation and Non-Human Intelligences encounters in his book, *Abduction.* Mack writes that the experience of "abduction" can lead to personal growth and transformation.

He lists the following as the results of contact:

- "Pushing through" occurs, i.e., fully experiencing the terror and rage associated with the helplessness and intrusive instrumentation of the ships. When this takes place, acknowledging and accepting the reality of the beings becomes possible, and a more reciprocal relationship follows in which personal growth and learning can occur. From the "ego death" follows other levels of transformation.
- The "aliens" (Mack's term) are recognized as intermediaries or intermediate entities between the fully embodied state of human beings and the primal source of creation or God (in the sense of cosmic consciousness, rather than a personified being). In this regard abductees (Mack's term) sometimes liken the alien beings to angels, or other "light beings" (including the "grays").
- The abductees (Mack's term) may experience themselves as returning to their cosmic source or "Home", an inexpressible beautiful realm beyond, or not in, space/time as we know it.
- Past lives are experienced during the sessions with strong emotion appropriate to what is being remembered.
- Past life experiences provide abductees with a different perspective about time and the nature

of human identity. Cycles of birth and death over long periods can thus be lived, providing a separate, less ego-derived sense of continuity of life and the smallness of individual life from a cosmic perspective. Consciousness is experienced as not coterminous with the body; the notion of a soul with an existence separate from the body becomes relevant.

· Once the separateness of consciousness from the body is grasped, other kinds of "transpersonal" experiences become possible; identification of consciousness with virtually infinite beings and entities through space/time and beyond often occurs.

· A distinct but essential aspect of this transpersonal experience is an abductee's sense of possessing a double human/alien identity.

· The reliving of abduction experiences leads abductees to open to other realities beyond space/time, realms that are variously described as beyond the "veil" or some additional barrier that has kept them in a box or a consciousness limited to the physical. When asked about these experiences, abductees have trouble finding the words to describe what has occurred and speak of the "collapse" of space/time, of the non-relevance of the notions of space and time, and being in multiple times and places at the exact moment. The result of all of these experiences are emotions of awe, respect for the mystery of nature, and a heightened sense of the sacredness of the natural world are along with a sense of sadness about the apparent hopelessness of Earth's environmental crisis.

Interestingly enough, The FREE Research Data reached very similar conclusions. The psychological profile changes from the FREE Research discovered that after the individual's contact experiences the following changes strongly increased:

- My concern with spiritual matters
- My desire to help others
- My compassion for others increased
- My appreciation of the ordinary things in life
- My ability to love others
- My insight into the problems of others
- My concern with the welfare of the planet
- My understanding of what life is about
- My concern with ecological matters
- My conviction that there is life after death

In addition, The FREE Research Data discovered:

- 75.4% believe that there is a connection between Non-Human Intelligences and Reincarnation.
- 82.5% believe that there is a connection between Non-Human Intelligences and the so-called "Spirit World."

- 25% were told by Non-Human Intelligences that they at one time were of a Non-Human Intelligence.
- 82% believe that Non-Human Intelligences can travel to the past and the future.
- 97% believe that Non-Human Intelligences can travel to "other dimensions."
- 24% were told that they had interacted with a Non-Human Intelligence in a past life.
- 38% believe that Non-Human Intelligences are "Modern Angels."
- 31% were given a message about what the experiencers called "*God.*"
- 91% believe that there is a grand plan in motion that Experiencers are all a part of.

We hear so much about the fear, the loathing, the scapegoating, and the xenophobia about the so-called "others," whether they be earthlings or off-world intelligences, that those at FREE (Foundation for Research into Extraterrestrial Encounters) wanted to tell another side of the story. For the record, The FREE organization is not a ufology organization. Instead, their focus is to explore the possible nature of "Consciousness" by examining the role and impact these extraordinary encounters with "Non-Human Intelligences" have on one's reported spiritual and behavioral transformations after the fact.

As you may have already gathered, much if not all of the above information may seem a bit too occult for most religious denominations here in the West, and for the scientific mainstream, who cling to outdated theories. Perhaps what is needed is a fusion of both science and religion or spirituality, something that appears many non-human intelligent civilizations have come to grips with eons ago. It seems that Einstein was correct when he said that science without religion is lame and that religion without science is blind.

There are three sides to a story; yours, mine, and the truth. We will leave that for you as the reader to decide. I want to share a brief conversation between the East Indian sage Ramana Maharshi and one of his students. The question posed to Maharshi was how we should treat others? His reply was, "There are no others." That appears to be the message being brought to us by many of these Non-Human Intelligences. Star People often tell us that we as human beings fear so much; we fight too much. We are destroying this beautiful planet of ours. What is required of us appears to be a different way of thinking, eventually leading to a different way of being. In other words, we need a change in consciousness. As a wise rabbi once said, "You do not pour new wine into old wineskins." (Matthew 9:17). And as Einstein quipped, problems are never solved by the same consciousness that created them in the first place.

Chapter Ten

In Their Own Words: Experiencer Stories

I have found a desire within myself that no experience in this world can satisfy; the most probable explanation is that I was made for another world.
- C.S. Lewis

Introduction

The contact stories that I am sharing are by people who appear to have achieved both a new way of thinking and a new way of being in the world. As we mature and evolve individually and collectively as a species, we will accept the foundational Universal Law - Life is change.

In whatever way this change occurs, one eventually

begins to see beyond the so-called 'reality of this world, with all of its laws of scarcity, fear, conformity, and illusion. Before the transformational experience, one "sees through a glass darkly." But then, somehow, clarity is restored. We move from the illusion of certainty to the certainty of illusion, as in the movie, "The Matrix". The mind once stretched by a new idea never returns to its original dimensions, Oliver Wendell Holmes reminds us. Once we see past the illusions of separateness and divisiveness, we can acknowledge the interconnectedness of all life. Everything we think and do affects every other being on the planet and even the multiverse.

We may ask ourselves, how could we have been so blind for so long? The Eureka moment, the "aha moment," has arrived. We discover that getting older is inevitable, but maturing is optional.

Remember that science, technology, and spirituality have grown at different rates in our lifetimes. Perhaps what is needed is a fusion of both science and spirituality, which appears many non-human intelligent civilizations have come to grips with eons ago. Albert Einstein was correct when he said that science without religion is lame and that religion without science is blind.

Carolyn's Story:

Carol is a retired English teacher from Alabama. The following is her story in her own words:

"*By the mid -1980s I had moved away from the fundamentalist ideas I had been taught as a child to a more abstract concept of God. Still, on this morning I sat on my bed and flippantly asked about this Jesus Christ. What kind of power does he have? Immediately a flash of lightning hit the inside of my head with such force that I almost fell back. My mind filled with a vision of floating angels, in the white-robed traditional garb, singing songs of praise. My mouth moved involuntarily, and I began to utter the most beautiful psalms and praise to God, and I knew while this was happening that I could not possibly compose these words. They were not coming from me. Then another vision filled my head. There were two rows of beings in vertical lines to the left and the right, standing as if they were at attention. They wore what looked like the short, armored outfit of a Roman gladiator. I felt myself walking through the middle of the two rows going up the flanks. The vision, however, abruptly stooped; and for the next 30 years, I would refer to these beings as warrior angels, and I constantly searched to get an understating of what they were.*

Meanwhile, the morning of strangeness had not finished. I jumped off the bed, chastising myself for being so impudent, so disrespectful. I grabbed my tennis racket and headed for a nearby court. I was by myself practicing my serve. My racket was in the back scratch position when another bolt of lightning flashed through my brain, and for no reason, I began to cry uncontrollably for the next three hours. Also, for the next three days or so, I became remarkably psychic, but it didn't last long. I knew this to be a "quickening" of some sort and remained silent about it all.

However, this event caused me to go through a phase of devotion that I never experienced for about a year, and truthfully I wish I could get it back. It took thirty plus years to finally get an inkling of what these "warrior angels" could possibly be. I was walking in my neighborhood when I met a couple of Latter Day Saint missionaries, the two young men no older than their early twenties, who had been canvassing the neighborhood. I have no idea what prompted me to tell them about the "warrior angels," but one of them, without hesitating, said, "Those are the Watchers."

Yes, the Watchers. Wasn't there an E.T. book by that name? I left the boys quickly, but they found my house anyway. However, in the course of their visit, I was able to examine some of the Latter Day Saint writings. I actually came across the "warrior angels" or "Watchers" in one of their writings. The writer did not use those terms, but it was a description of a vision exactly like mine. This is what was said about the vision: it is the path of a mystic."

Carolyn then provided us with a second experience. This one is unique because Carolyn had no interest in science fiction or ufology before this second story. It reminds me of my contact experiences because before my contacts, I too had no interest in science fiction or the study of UFOs. I had never even watched a Star Wars film or Star Trek until many years into having contact. It simply didn't interest me.

Carolyn goes on to say:

"This event occurred around the early 1990s or perhaps late 1980s. I must first explain that even though I had many flashes of images and memories of an extraterrestrial nature from childhood, these images would fade into a cloudy part of my brain so that I would not think about them. Sometimes, when my mind drifted toward those things, a hypnotic voice would say, "Don't think about it... Don't think about it," and I simply wouldn't. It all disappeared into some fog. So when I say that I took no interest in "aliens" at the time, hard to believe but true...I truly didn't.

However, there was a fellow that my husband and I met who amused us with all kinds of strange stories, and he got his information from a UFO convention. At the time, my husband and I enjoyed Star Trek, so when we learned that there was a UFO convention in Gulf Breeze, Florida, we decided to explore the panhandle and check out the convention while we were there... and check out the crazy people.

The morning of the trip, I packed and ironed my hus-

band's shirts. As I was pressing down on a stubborn, wrinkled collar, a voice filled my head. It was loud, determined, forceful, and it would let up. "Who are you? Who are you?" I felt as if I was being shaken, roughed up to get something out of me from the very core of my being. "Who are you?" I had to say something, and I came out with the ridiculous statement straight out of Marvel Comics. "I am the keeper of the flame."

"Keeper of the flame, you belong to us," the voice responded in a more paternal tone. The next thing that I remember is that three hours later, we were barreling up 175, headed north at about 75 miles an hour.

I did not sleep. I never do when someone else is driving. But I blinked. I was in the presence of a creature with big black eyes who seemed to float closer and closer to me until we were eyeball to eyeball. At the next moment, I was there in the passenger seat, still speeding up the highway. I never told my husband about this or the voice during ironing. It all just settled into that foggy place in the back of my head that I didn't question. The convention lobby was filled with Whitley Streiber's Communion, and there was that same creature on the front cover who had closed in eyeball to eyeball.

After that, everything moved from that foggy back of my mind to crystal clarity. I remembered everything. I could connect the dots. On that day, someone had carefully orchestrated a great realization within me. From then on, I knew myself to be a contactee with *something important to say. I pursued spirituality, psychic development, mediumship, remote viewing, everything dealing with consciousness. In one day, someone pulled me off one life path to another. Someone decided I was ready.*

.

My Commentary:

In a phone conversation with Carolyn before writing this section, she told me that she felt as if a fog had lifted after this experience. She began to see images from the past and remembered her contacts when she was a little girl. Carolyn has moved on from the study ufology to primarily consciousness studies. At the beginning of her narrative, Carolyn mentioned "The Watchers." These beings have been involved with the history of our planet for thousands of years. They are mentioned by name in The Book of Enoch in chapter 12 verses 2, 4, and 5 when Enoch writes:

"And behold the Watchers called me Enoch the scribe."

And in verse number 4 he writes:

"Then the Lord said to me: Enoch, scribe of righteousness, go tell the Watchers of heaven, who have deserted the lofty sky, and their holy everlasting station, who have been polluted with women..."

Verse 4 begins a more detailed account of the Genesis 6 narrative, telling the story about the "Sons of God" coming down to earth and having sexual relations with earth women.

These beings are also mentioned in the Apocryphal Old Testament book entitled, *The Book of Jubilees,* where a more detailed version of the Genesis story of Adam and Eve is being told. For the record, the word *apocryphal* means doubtful authenticity; however, when reading these stories, one begins to get an uneasy feeling as to why these books never made it into the biblical canon.

Last but not least, author and researcher Raymond Fowler, working with the famous experiencer Betty Andreasson, has written two books about these beings. The first is titled, *The Watchers* and the second volume is appropriately titled, *The Watchers 2.* Betty Andreasson is a devout Christian, and her interpretation of her encounters reflects her faith tradition's perspective and theology. That is the lens through which she views her contactee experiences.

Many experiencers have maintained their Christian religious faith, incorporating their faith into their contact experiences. Then, those Experiencers have found that the traditional Christian story does not resonate with them once they have had contact with non-human intelligences. There is no conflict in this, for it is more about how one lives their life as opposed to what one believes. I know what you believe by how you treat other human beings and the planet. In short, how you live your life will speak volumes, or as a wise rabbi once noted, "By their fruit, you shall know them." (Matthew 7: 15-20).

Also notable is a wonderful book by the author Brad Steiger who has been in the trenches of UFO research for decades. One of the first books I read after my initial contact experiences was Mr. Steiger's book, *The Fellowship*. It is an excellent work about the spiritual contact between human beings and Non-Human Intelligences. I recommend it highly.

Jamie's Story

Jamie is a 35-year-old computer programmer and visual artist, born in Texas and now residing in Illinois.

.

"There I lay. A small child alone in a dark room petrified with fear. My imagination running out of control with the fearful imagery of what I may see come out of the sky to take me away. This is not the start of an extraterrestrial abduction story, but instead my childhood fears after some intense church sermons. The pastor's voice would boom as his fists pounded the pulpit; preaching with such conviction the bible stories about the "end times" and the return of Jesus. As if this wasn't scary enough for my little mind to take in, I also heard that God drowned a whole earth full of people of all ages, and even killed innocent Egyptian kids in their sleep one night. I was truly a God-fearing child.

By the time I was 15 years old, religious matters or spirituality of any kind was not on my mind much at all, if ever. My thoughts were overloaded with what I thought were major life concerns; pimples, math tests, if I looked like a total dork to the guy I had a major crush on. At this impressionable age came my first conscious memory of seeing intelligent beings that were not human. I woke up at an unknown time of night to see that I was in a very bright place with several white beings with large black eyes looking down at me. Total terror washed over me. Then as quick as it began, it all ended. My eyes closed, and I was unconscious until morning where I found myself in bed as if nothing had ever happened. This was a very different dream, and I knew it. So what do I do but nightly start watching "Unsolved Mysteries" on T.V. to catch the latest episodes of fear-filled accounts of alien abductions. I was desperate to understand anything about what I had experienced.

On through my 20s and early 30s, my life was barren spiritually. My first child came as a wonderful surprise at the age of 30. My spiritual life began to blossom, and in 2012 I found an uplifting church with an inspirational preacher, and I came to a point when I decided I really needed to quiet my mind from outer distractions. I had a regular prayer life, and then the visits began again in full force. The experiences happen in my home. Some are in a strange altered state in the middle of the night. Many, however, occur when I am fully aware and awake.

So here I am astral traveling, having a kundalini experience, and lucid dreaming. To my mind, experiencers are like spiritual Galileos. People back in his day thought the earth was the center of the solar system and everything revolved around us. He discovered that this was not true but was scorned, ridiculed, and shamed by others and was threatened by the Church. All this because he had an open and brilliant mind and could understand a truth that other people could not. Should we seek comfort or should we seek truth?

Every thought, word, and action emotion is based on one of two things—love or fear. Whatever form we need to think of God as being to make us comfortable enough to evolve and understand is ok for now. Whatever we need for now to move us out from fear into love is a good thing. Whether we think of God as a creative life-giving energy, a human-looking form, is okay...it is what it is no matter how we choose to think about it. So we can argue all we want over our different perspectives, it really doesn't matter. Those fear-based emotions separate us even more from each other and this divine force.

What are these beings here for, and why are they contacting me? I still can't answer that one. Just knowing about telepathy, different energies, astral travel, altered states of consciousness, all this has taken me to a level of spirituality and understanding that I never even knew was possible. I have so much to learn. They have lifted me out to of the fear-based spiritually and barren place that I was in, into a now incredibly spiritual and connected place."

My Commentary:

Jamie's story speaks for itself regarding a new way of thinking and being in the world after her contact experiences. A spiritual transformation has indeed occurred. It is also worth noting that Jamie has experienced quite a few of the contact characteristics according to the FREE Research Survey. Jamie feels her experiences changed her life for the better. According to FREE research, 50.9% responded that their contacts positively affected changing their lives. 85% of individuals said they had interacted with these beings more than once. Jamie has interacted with them on more than one occasion. Another important factor is that 81% of those who participated in the Phase 1 FREE Survey have reported an out of body experience or OBE. 35% of our participants stated that a physical non-human intelligence appeared to them as a child, and 84% reported very vivid or lucid dreams. It seems that Jamie has hit the jackpot.

Rey's Story:

This next narrative is from Mr. Reinerio (Rey) Hernandez. Mr. Hernandez is a Co-Founder of FREE, CO-Chair of the Free Research Committee, Experiencer, Former University Professor, and currently a Tax Attorney with the United States Internal Revenue Service. He has had numerous experiences involving NDEs (Near Death Experiences) and contact with Non- Human Intelligences, but rarely talks about it publicly. These experiences transformed him from atheism to a deeply felt spirituality and the "Oneness" of all creation. I want to be clear here that I, nor the FREE Organization (Foundation for Research into Extraterrestrial and Extraordinary Experiences) is in any way implying that a transformation from atheism to any form of spirituality or religion is the highest stage of evolution a human being can obtain. We are noting the increased occurrences of people undergoing this type of inner transformation after such contacts with non-human intelligences. Here is a portion of Rey's story after he and his wife had an experience with a being of light in March of 2012.

"Here is another magical incident, after my wife and I had the experience with a light being in March of 2012. I was the rational materialist atheist who was never exposed to the topic of UFOs prior to this contact, spent hours upon hours on the internet and ordered a ton of books on the topic of UFOs. All this accomplished was to confuse me even more. Even after reading all of these UFO books, I still remained an atheist. All of this changed after my August 2012 encounter with yet another craft.

In August of 2012, 6 months after our encounter

with the energy being in our living room, I playfully called down a large craft that was also seen by my daughter and three friends. This craft was the size of a small football stadium, around 100 meters by 600 meters, and hovered less than five feet from the roof of my neighbor's house for 45 minutes.

The very next day after this experience, I immediately stopped searching the internet and purchasing books on Amazon. Instead, I began to order and read over three hundred books on Near-Death Experiences.

For 3 months, I was reading NDE books, 18 hours per day. It was an obsession. I neglected my job and family and spent all of my time reading NDE Books until December 21, 2012.

All of this changed on December 21, 2012. For 3 days in a row, the very first 3 individuals I had ever mentioned NDEs to, Dec 21-23, for 3 days in a row, all three had an NDE. What are the statistical odds of this happening? This series of events lead to my spiritual transformation.

On December 21, 2012, my daughter developed a high fever and I brought her to our pediatrician who is originally from Colombia. We discovered that my daughter had an ear infection and all of the sudden I had an uncontrollable urge to tell the doctor about the topic of NDEs.

I recall asking the doctor in a robotic voice, "Excuse me Doctor, but have you ever heard of Near-Death Experiences? I have just finished reading 300 books on this topic, and I estimate that at least 30 medical doctors have written about this topic area, and many of these doctors are professors in medical schools. Thus NDEs have been scientifically studied and validated and this is something that you need to be aware of.' Part of my was mind was conscious and another part of my mind was saying to me "Stop, what are you doing, why are you asking this question?"

The doctor's response was how did you know I had an NDE? The doctor was shocked and her eyes were popping out of her head and she proceeded to tell me the story about the NDE and being outside of her body watching and listening to what was going on. The doctor told me that she had a heart attack and was declared clinically dead at a hospital in Colombia.

On Saturday, December 22, 2012, while having dinner with another couple at a Catholic Church, a similar event occurred. While speaking to a friend at dinner who was a radiological technician at a nearby hospital, I once again blurted out the same comment I made to the doctor about NDEs and the scientific studies validating them. I did this word for word as I did with the doctor, and this man was a total stranger. His response was almost identical to the doctor's response—shock and disbelief.

He told me the story of his mother dying in his arms and being pronounced clinically dead for 30 minutes

She was revived at a nearby hospital, and when she recovered, she told him about her NDE and her out-of-body experience. She described what was going on as she hovered over the scene where her "death" had occurred. She described the appearances of the paramedics and traveling through a tunnel with a bright light that got larger and larger as she got closer to it. She said she entered this light and saw her deceased husband in spirit form and that they embraced upon seeing each other. She was later told by an entity which she described as "God" that she had to go back to earth and that it was not her time although she said she wanted to stay.

On Sunday, December 23rd, 2012, I went to visit my parents, who were both in their mid-80s at the time. My father is very ill and bedridden most of the time. While talking, I mentioned to him the stories I heard from the pediatrician and the radiological technician because I always thought my father was an atheist. Imagine my surprise when my father told me about his NDE, which happened about 15 years before.

It was the classic story, floating above his body, watching the doctors and nurses attempt to save his life. He saw and heard everything. Finally the tunnel and the light, seeing deceased loved ones, in this case, his parents and his brother in spirit form. They embraced. His decease family members introduced him to an entity he identified as "God." There was also a life *review which he described as lasting "20-30 years" He told me that time does not exist, that Hell does not exist, and that God was pure Love and that we are here on Earth to learn.*

That Sunday evening, while driving home from my parent's home, I spoke to GOD for the first time. I looked up at the stars and said to both God and the Entities, I congratulate you---you have managed to completely transform a total atheist into someone who does not believe, but actually "knows" that God exists, that we are eternal spiritual beings, and that there is in fact "life after death" I have this belief more than any Catholic priest in Miami. I still believe this to this day. This NDE story is just one of the many clear examples of the many "synchronicities" in my life that I have experienced since I started my E.T. contact experiences."

My Commentary:

What is notable about Rey's experience is that he also displayed what we would call psychic abilities after his contacts. What are the chances that the first three individuals he has ever spoken to about NDEs would all state that they had NDEs. Also, what are the chances of this occurring on three consecutive days, Friday, Saturday, and Sunday? I have met three patients during my six years of work as a professional chaplain who have talked to me of their NDEs, but it was years in between them.

The Eastern Traditions, especially but not limited to Hindus and Buddhists, acknowledge that psychic (paranormal) abilities are a natural outcome as one progresses to achieve states of consciousness that result in transcendence and religious experience. They also warn that these should not become ends in themselves. The monotheistic religions are based on the teachings of a few individuals. They are described as prophets, saints, or rishis, and all of these teachings are based on the intensely personal experiences of those individuals

Religious experience, the mystic experience, the peak experience all have one thing in common. Those are the encounters with pure consciousness. There is no subject-object distinction, no content but a transformational process that often results in remarkable behavioral changes and beliefs and sometimes translates into informational content. Perhaps the philosopher William James is correct when he states that "the mother sea and fountain-head of all religions lies in the mystical experiences of the individual." If so, we would do well to heed his words and pay close attention, especially regarding the individual who has had contact with non-human intelligent beings and has undergone a spiritual/religious transformation.

Below is a selected summary from the Phase 2 FREE Experiencers Survey data from April 10, 2017.

After the first year of contact:

82% said their concern for spiritual matters had increased.

16% said their concern for spiritual matters has stayed the same.

3% said their concern for spiritual matters had decreased.

75% said their desire to help others increased.

80% said that their compassion for others had increased.

75% said that they felt there was a connection between reincarnation and Extraterrestrials.

54% said they were given a message of universal love and oneness.

Does this sound familiar? With the exception of reincarnation, they are themes that run throughout this book. Now we will continue with more Experiencers words.

Debra's Story:

Now let us consider the experience of Debra Kauble. Debra is a factory worker in Indiana. Initially, she did not see her contacts as positive experiences. Some of you readers may know her as "Kathy Davis", the experiencer from Budd Hopkin's book *Intruders*. I have spoken to Kathy over the phone and via Skype, and I find her to be one of the most unpretentious, genuine, and insightful people I have ever met. To know more about her experiences, you must read the book, but I want to share with you where she is now regarding the things that have happened to her.

Below is her response to FREE Co-Founder Rey Reinerio's post on Facebook, asking if her experiences had changed her spiritually.

"That would be a great big YES! My name is Debbie Jordan Kauble, but most people know me as Kathy Davis from Budd Hopkin's book, Intruders. I have always said that the night of June 30, 1983, Debbie died, and I was born—or reborn, if you will. From that point on, something in my mind and my heart opened up. I began to realize the connection I had with ALL life; All Life EVERYWHERE (emphasis Debra's)

I began to realize what I was and what we really are. I am not a human on a spiritual journey, I am a spirit on a human journey. All these thoughts and feelings came flooding in. It was at this time that I also began to realize what death was to me, and I began my adventures into paranormal research; connecting with the "other side."And not just people who have passed but also other dimensions and times. I realize it may sound crazy "God" as a being splintered into an infinite number of shards of light and each life form is a beautiful manifestation of that light. That life light Is each of us. ALL living things. EVERYWHERE.

I was raised by a Catholic dad and a Protestant mom; neither went to church. I had the basics of Christianity and went to various churches with different school friends as a kid. I would have always said I believed in God and that Jesus was who he said he was, and that my relationship with them was nobody's business, and I don't take direction or judgment from any man (like the Pope). I was sassy and strong-willed (still am).

I just wanted to share that with you and would be curious to see if anyone else felt this too.
Sincerely,
Deb. Kauble

My Commentary:

It is important to note that this transformation did not occur immediately in Debra's case; for some, it does; for others, it does not. It is a process, which is what spiritual growth or transformation entails. That is part of the reason that Dr. Edgar Mitchell, the co-founder of the FREE Foundation and founder of the Institute of Noetic Sciences, has as FREE's mission "What is Consciousness" by undertaking cross-comparative research on individuals that have had contact with Non-Human Intelligence (NHI) via the "Contact Modalities." Contact via perceived UFOs, NDEs, OBEs,

Remote Viewing, Channeling, Ghosts/Spirits, Hallucinogenic Journeys, Orbs, PSI Contact, and so on.

In an interview with FREE Co-Founder Rey Hernandez, Dr. Mitchell discusses E.T. Contact and the need to establish friendly relations with them because we may need their assistance in the future. The interview date was March 2, 2015. Dr. Mitchell says that there is evidence to suggest that the E.T.'s have been visiting us for centuries and that they have a better working knowledge of how the universe works than we do at this time.

He also says that he has personal connections around the globe with people who are all on the same page regarding this phenomenon. Dr. Mitchell acknowledges that these beings are from different solar systems, different planets and that they have solved the technical problems of traveling through time and space.

Dr. Mitchell says that the more information we can apply from Experiencers to the science we now possess (always knowing that we are growing and evolving scientifically), the better off we will be. He says that human beings must get to know the E.T.s better and get to know us better to create what he calls "workable relationships" with them. It is a fascinating interview from the sixth human being to walk on the moon.

My final Experiencer is Mr. Alberto A. Fernandez. Alberto's contacts are much too numerous to mention and could fill a book just by themselves. I was introduced to Alberto by Rey Hernandez and found him to be an extremely humble human person.

Alberto's Story:

My name is Alberto A. Fernandez. I was born 5/21/ 1945 in the city of Santiago de Cuba in the oriental region of Cuba. My parents had been married around 5 years when I was born, and they both had a 3-year-old boy named Carlos. My mother (Lydia Sotera) was a beloved teacher and my father, Carlos Alberto Fernandez Baquero, a wealthy, very good-looking businessman and also a womanizer. I always heard their marriage was in turmoil but my mom was madly in love with him. I was born prematurely, and unfortunately, my mother died four days after my birth due to postpartum septicemia. She was only 27 years old. My father showed up in the hospital 4 hours after her death. After this tragic event, my father abandoned my brother and me; he left Cuba and remarried overseas, and never cared for us afterward. On her death bed, my mother, Lydia, told her godmother and aunt, Maria Gonzalez D'Estrade, (a 56-year-old widower), to take care of me, and she did so all her life. My brother was sent to live with another relative.

It was during these times that I experienced my first paranormal experiences. I was around two or three years old when I witnessed a man filled with light in a white robe sitting on my bed and tenderly patting my head while he was watching me play. I did not know this man at all. Years later, I saw a painting of Jesus, and I felt a deep connection with him; this was the man who tenderly patted my head and watched me play years before. One evening, when I was six years old, I was in my bedroom by myself when suddenly the lights went off. It was pitch black. Suddenly, a bright light appeared in front of me out of nowhere. This light had an ignited heart within it. The light was hovering approximately a foot from my chest. This ignited, red heart slowly got closer and closer to my chest, when entered my chest I started to convulse. Sometime later, I saw a drawing of Jesus depicting the ignition inside of the sacred heart of Jesus Christ.

This intense image gave me a 'déja vu' of the experience I had as a child. I have not witnessed anything like that again in my life. When I was around six, my mom and I move to Habana (The Capital of Cuba). Maria's only daughter had married a wealthy, miserly man. He was going to provide me with schooling so my mom to move with them. We were both treated like servants and emotionally abused. My life was very tormented during these times. The children of the couple, Olga Marin and Micky, were close to me.

By the age of 14, I had a near-death experience, I was swimming at the Casino Deportivo, a family beach resort northern coast of Havana. I was playing in the peer by myself, and it occurred to me to jump off a

16 feet peer into the open ocean. Suddenly, I realized I was caught in a strong rip current. I didn't know how to avoid it or swim to the shore. I tried fighting it, for a long time until I became very tired and had no more strength. I just gave up. I was drowning; I would see myself going down under the water. Flashes of my entire Life went through my mind, thoughts of my deceased mother Lydia and of God. I knew this was the end of my life. I remember I said, "Mother! God! Help me!" Suddenly, almost in a flash, I felt a tremendous force, like immense energy, that pulled me out of the depths and gently placed me on the concrete sidewalk of the peer. I did not have a scratch! I did not even cough up any water! I was in such a state of shock that I stood up immediately and walked home. I did not tell anyone about this incident. I even thought I kind of forgot about it until years later. It was explained to me I was a 'walk in'.

By the age of sixteen, I migrated to the United States as a part of the Peter Pan program. In this program, over 14,000 Cuban children were sent to the United States without their families. It was a huge rumor on the Island that the government was going to take sole custody of the children instead of their parents. In a state of panic, the parents will send their children in planes to the USA with the hope to reunite with them in weeks. This did not happen because Castro closed the right to leave the country. After this, some children were separated from their parents for years. I did not see my mother for six years. These children were placed in different foster homes throughout Miami.

By eighteen, I joined the U.S. Army in a special program to fight against the Cuban regime. This program was discontinued after the assassination of President John F. Kennedy. I finished my service and returned to Miami. I then got married and joined the Metro-Dade Police Department in 1969.

In 1973, while I was driving home after finishing my shift around 11:30 pm. As I opened the front gate of my home, I suddenly noticed on my right-hand side a bright beam of light coming down from what appeared to be a helicopter. I soon realized that it wasn't a helicopter because it didn't sound like one. The craft was shaped like a hamburger with a bright blue light. It rotated counterclockwise with a red light on the top. A yellow light shined from inside the windows. It was flying right above the roof of my house. I ran inside to call my wife at the time, and the sound of the craft also woke up my next-door neighbor.

This phenomenon tampered with my brain. I wasn't the same individual after this encounter. Years later, I found out there was a missing time during this occurrence. From 1973 up to 1987, something strange started happening to me. I would wake up in the middle of the night, sensing the presence of an entity in my bedroom. This energy would start paralyzing me from my feet to my head. This unknown energy possessed my body and my mind. I had no control over it. I was in terror every night because I couldn't scream. In 1987, these occurrences were explained to me through an encounter of a third kind with a grey female alien being years later.

After serving years as a police officer, I went back to school to become a DEA agent and in 1984 I was assigned as a U.S. diplomat to the U.S. embassy in the Dominican Republic as second in command in the DEA office. While on duty, I got injured and returned to Miami (By this time, I had already remarried and had my youngest daughter). We stayed temporarily at the Penthouse Sofitel Hotel in Miami; the room was big with two big, super-strong tempered glass windows facing the southwest.

One evening (approximately 11 pm), the fire alarm of the hotel went off. At first, many hotel guests came out of their rooms. The management explained it was a false alarm; when we returned to our room, my beeper started to shake and randomly vibrate; the electricity flickered on and off. The super-thick glass windows started to shake intensely like if they were made out of plastic. This all happened while I was lying on the bed wide awake with my wife (my 1-year-old infant daughter slept quietly in the crib while all this was happening). Suddenly, an unknown creature appeared floating in front of my bed. (my wife was apparently hypnotized and fell asleep suddenly without witness my en-

counter. I was witnessing a solid, three-dimensional, grey, dolphin skinned creature approximately three feet tall with a big head, no hair, huge black eyes,(no pupils no sclera), black tiny nose and mouth, no ears, a long neck, long skinny arms to her side, long hands and fingers and nails, her facial expression was flat, no emotions. I was not scared but calm. This unknown creature talked to me telepathically telling me she was a female. She proceeded to explain that they have been collecting semen from me for years in order to help them in the procreation of their dying race and that my helping mission was completed with them.(In fact, she kept her promise, and I was never bothered again).

I have no recollection of what happened afterward, but years later, I was informed that I had consented to these procedures in a previous lifetime. I remember the next morning feeling still in shock; I had no idea what had happened to me. I felt very strange. I suddenly noticed I could see the aura of everyone around me.

The following day, I walked into a bookstore and saw the book "Communion" by Whitley Streiber (the creature on the cover book similar to the one I saw the night before). I purchased the book and read it avidly to find answers to what was happening to me. Years later, this experience was filmed and put on air in a documentary on Spanish CNN (Infinito Program). Researching about these paranormal encounters has changed my life. Never before did this kind of subject matter interest me.

I desperately searched for people or groups that held similar experiences. I thought I was going crazy then, I joined 'Contacto 12' group around 1987, as well as "RAMA" based in Lima, Peru, and directed by Sixto Paz-Wells. These groups, their participants, and practices continue to help me to understand my experiences. In 1988, during a RAMA UFO world encounter, the Chilca dessert, Peru I experienced going through a "Xendra" a paranormal effect consisting of passing into another dimension. A UFO craft projected a bluish neon beam of light towards the ground. When I entered this beam, I saw it was a blue kaleidoscope on the ground. Suddenly a beam of bright white light came from nowhere at a 45 angle, and the Holy grail appeared in front of me. Immediately after, 12 light beings came out from this same light. They were 12 bearded white monks dressed in brown robes, all with a rope tied around their waists.

A few years later (in Mt. Shasta California) it was explained to me that these monks were the guardians of the Holy Grail. I also witnessed colorful lights on my ceiling and wall bedroom at night (like a disco place). I had new experiences of this sort that started to happen almost daily in my life. On one occasion, I recall entering my house and seeing a tall bright Nordic-like man dressed in a light white uniform. He had slanted big green eyes and long straight blondish white hair. He suddenly disappeared without a trace. Advanced math, physics formulas, and equations came to me, which I had no clue of and could not recall the next day. I wit-

nessed my bedroom room filled with fog one night, I was awakened from my sleep, and an enlightened being with oriental creatures was telling me to "go back to sleep, I'm talking to your subconscious mind."

In another of these intensive and busy nights, at approximately 11:50 pm, I felt strong energy pulling me and lifting me from my bed like being sucked up. A bright light appeared in front of me; I was very frightened, but without explanation, the light and the scary feeling disappeared. When I woke up the next morning, I could hardly see. I went to an optometrist nearby sunset and ninety-nine. He asked me, "Were you exposed to a bright light lately?" Of course, I said a big "NO!" He then proceeded to tell me that I had a triangle shape on each pupil of my eyes. We were both puzzled.

These kinds of unique experiences continued over the course of my life. I remember a Holy Friday when I bled profusely from my right eye. I also remember on another Holy Friday, I was wearing a white T-shirt and a bloody serum started to ooze from my chest staining my white T-shirt. Sometimes, a silver medallion that I would wear on my neck would turn gold and vice versa; or a crucifix would bleed and even smell like blood during Holy Friday.

My wife, who is a clinical psychologist, would witness these phenomena as well. One night, I was awakened from my sleep by a dialogue between what I would consider two or more aliens. They were conversing with each other on my balcony; and their voices sounded guttural like a strange Nordic language was coming from 'a box'. On this occasion, I looked outside my balcony, and from under my bedroom curtain, I saw feet moving and walking outsider. The balcony was lit with neon lights (my balcony was approximately 14 stories high, facing the ocean). There was no access to go up from any angles; no one from this planet could have come up and walked back and forth on that Miami Beach balcony. These entities were real and were talking to each other. I was very much awake, but once again, I turned back around in my bed and continue sleeping like nothing happened.

The next morning, my wife and my youngest daughter (at the time she was eighteen) confirmed they also saw bright neon lights on the balcony and felt people talking on the balcony. In this same apartment, we observed a UFO craft, and my wife and my daughter and I were sitting on the balcony around 6 pm having a trivial conversation when suddenly, we all saw a metallic disc-shaped UFO traveling from North Miami Beach to South Beach over the Atlantic Ocean, It was close to the shore, that my daughter was able to see the windows and lights inside the craft. This craft glided into the water and disappeared without a trace. My wife stated later that she wanted to go inside to get a camera and take a photo, but she realized the craft was moving too fast, so she decided to count slowly in her mind.

She later told us that it took the craft 6 seconds to

make it from North Beach to South Beach, where we all saw it gliding into the water without any splash (an estimate of over 70 blocks in 6 seconds).

With regards to Jesus, I forgot to mention several other vivid personal experiences. As a child, I remembered suddenly being transported to the past. I was not dreaming but very awake. I witness Jesus standing on a big rock teaching to a large group of people; I could see him on my right side as I felt part of this crowd. Days later, while watching historical events of Jesus on the Discovery Channel.

I revised my visions when they recreated Jesus teaching at the sermon on the mountain. I said to myself, "I was there with him". On another occasion, when I was visiting a friend, suddenly I saw a black dot appearing in space. To my surprise, the dot turned into the face of Jesus with his crown of thorns. He was observing me with deep brownish eyes. I was able to observe in detail all his facial features, even his pores. His skin was olive, his beard was uneven, and his nose was broken at the bridge of the nose. The face suddenly disappeared after a while; I was in such a state of shock after this experience that I couldn't speak for two days. That face, those eyes, and that look are still in my mind always. Another day, while relaxing in my chair, I was able to see the image of a long cave, and a voice told me, "This is how Jesus was born." I saw the moment of his birth.

From within the cave, a bright flashing light illuminated the entire cave! It was so impressive.

On another occasion, a person wanted me to put my hands over her for healing. I always had doubts when it comes to these affairs. Although I know it is God and not me who heals, I asked God for confirmation. That same day, while looking out at the blue sky, I saw a figure of a man in a gold, long robe; it was sister Faustina's Jesus of the mercy where beams of light white and red were pouring from his palms. I called the person and told her to pray to Jesus, and the prayers were answered, and she got better. One day my nephew told me that on several occasions, he would see a white young man in a white robe with a beard next to me; my nephew confirmed that one of the drawings of Jesus his mother had in her room was the one he would see walking with me around his house. These particular drawings looked like the Jesus illustrated in the movie "Heaven is for Real."

Another touchy experience I never forgot, was in the '90s when I went grocery shopping with my youngest daughter. A young male in his 30's was next to my window; as I parked my car, he was holding the hand of his young daughter (a beautiful blonde girl around four years old), and he said to me that he and his daughter were hungry. Trained as a law enforcement officer, I am always aware of my surroundings. This man came out of nowhere, which surprised me quite a bit. I personally felt somewhat upset because I was caught off-guard. He was dressed in jeans, appeared to be around 6 feet tall, 190 lbs" white skin with a beard.

Both he and the girl looked unkempt. I told him to go with me inside the grocery store, and I proceeded to tell him to buy anything he needed & that I was going to pay for his items. He did not speak a word anymore. After I purchased the groceries, he and the little girl walked outside. I walked to my car, and they were in front of me, but when I opened the car to seat my daughter in the backseat, they disappeared! I looked everywhere in the parking lot for them, but there was no sign of them.

I was very puzzled, but when I saw the movie "Heaven is for Real" years later, I realized that the young man I saw with the little girl was Jesus. The Jesus of the movie was dressed identically to the one I saw that day.

On another occasion, I was resting in my Miami Beach apartment suddenly; I felt an urgency to go to my brother's Carlos house on the other side of town. I keep feeling very strange while I was at Carlos's house when his friend (J) arrived with a lot of pain in his knees; he said he was going to have knee surgery the following week.

I intuitively felt to go outside to do a "Sun Ceremony" we all saw the sun dancing, suddenly Carlos start to scream because a beam of light came down from the sun towards his chest and burned him, leaving *a permanent mark that he still carries as of today. Meanwhile, I put my hands over J's Knees and gave him energy, his pain went away, and he ended up not having the surgery. I felt more comfortable after everything that happened at Carlo's and disclosed to me that the night before two entities of light appeared to him and told him to go the next day to Carlo's because his brother "Alberto" was going to be used as an instrument of healing.*

There are countless manifestations and experiences that have been happening in my life that I haven't mentioned in this narrative, but I plan to write more in the future. For now, I just keep believing that anything is possible, and we should not laugh about the things we don't know because there is so much we don't know!

The Big Question

One of the difficulties when reading or studying this phenomenon is that it is so subjective. Yes, that is true; and yet so many individuals are reporting the same sorts of experiences. The high strangeness of it and the subjectivity of the experiences can be mind-boggling. Perhaps Star People are challenging us to redefine what reality is and what it means. Yet eventually, the question becomes, how do we best prepare ourselves for the open presence of non-human intelligences contacting us?

First of all, a fearful and confused population is a controlled population. With all of the misinformation and distortion found in ufology today, the entire field becomes so scrambled that no one anywhere can put together a meaningful total overview. No mass confusion occurs by chance. So, therefore, we must ask ourselves why there has been so much concentrated effort to keep people off balance and confused?

Some people have much to lose should the entire truth of what is going on in our skies become common knowledge. So the question remains, how do we prepare ourselves for these non-human intelligences? Certainly not by stockpiling nuclear weapons in fear; after all, we most certainly would be outmatched in an aggressive response. Instead, let us draw upon the best inspiration and leadership that our wisest philosophers, our most revered religious leadership, our great progressive scientific minds, and the global political leadership that perhaps the United Nations can provide.

I don't think it should be left up to governments, whether democracies or dictatorships, to make our choices. We do not want to squander this opportunity.

After reading the messages from people who have been contacted, how do you feel? Does anything you have read tell you anything about the intelligences who have brought the messages to us? Do you agree with these viewpoints, or are they foreign to you and how you choose to see life and the world?

These experiences can serve as reminders to humankind. One of those reminders is that there are as many paths to God as there are people who walk those paths. Many Saints, Prophets, and Avatars have been sent to our planet to raise human spiritual consciousness down through the centuries.

Because of the nature of human oral and written history, it is difficult to say whether or not all of them are Non-Human Intelligences, yet one thing is sure. The message of oneness can be traced throughout humanity's religious and spiritual quests; it's just that we don't live it out very well as a collective. Perhaps that will change. Indeed it is my sincere hope and prayer that it will.

Human evolution is slow and tedious at times. But this book will likely not be considered blasphemy by many. There was a time when a book like this would not be received well at all, much less written. Victor Hugo was correct when he said that nothing is as powerful as an idea whose time has come.

A characteristic of any message of great import is that you can discern its truthfulness by your inner resonance. Does this book ring true to you? Are you ready and welcoming of our Visitors?

Appendix A

ORGANIZATIONS

- MUFON, (The Mutual UFO Network). Headquarters in Sequin, Texas. Established in 1969.

- CUFOS, The J. Allen Hynek Center for UFO Studies founded in 1973.

- FUFOR, The Fund for UFO Research, established in 1979.

- Ancient Astronaut Society, Highland Park, Illinois.

- CAUS, Citizens Against UFO Secrecy. Conducts Freedom of Information Acts inquiries to obtain government-held information on UFOs.

Appendix B

COUNSELING FOR EXPERIENCERS

- Dr. Richard J. Boylan, Ph.D. 2826 O Street, Suite 2. Sacramento, California, 95816. (916) 455-0120.
- Reverend Michael JS Carter, Asheville, North Carolina, michaeljscarter@gmail.com

- Dr. Aphrodite Clamar, 1108 Somerset Ave. Lakewood, NJ 08701. (800) 275-3243.

- Dr. Edith Fiore, Ph.D. 20688 Fourth Street, Saratoga, California, 95070. (408) 867-1100.

- Yvonne Smith, C.HT. Hypnotherapist for PTSD. yvonne4ptsd@gmail.com (818) 383-6903.

Appendix C

RECOMMENDED READING

Pioneers of Oneness: The Science and Spirituality of UFOs and *The Space Brothers* by Gerard Aartsen, BGA Publications, Amsterdam, The Netherlands, 2020. www.bgapublications.nl

Celestial Healing: Close Encounters That Cure by Virginia Aronson, Signet Publications, New York, NY.1999.

Inside The Flying Saucers by George Adamski, Warner Books, New York, NY.1955,

The Healing Power of UFOs: 300 True Accounts of People Healed by Extraterrestrials by Preston Dennett, Blue Giant Books, 2019.

Captured! The Betty and Barney Hill UFO Experience by Stanton T. Friedman and Kathleen Marden, Career Press, 2017.

Listening To Extraterrestrials: Telepathic Coaching by Enlightened Beings by Lisette Larkins, Hampton Roads Publishing, Charlottesville, Va. 2004.

The Contactees by Joseph Randazzo, UFO Library Limited, Studio City, California, 1993.

UFOs: A Great New Dawn For Humanity, by Enrique, Castillo Rincon, Blue Dolphin Publishing, Nevada City, California, 1997.

The Invitation by Sixto Paz Wells, 1st World Library, Fairfield, IA,1997. 1st World Library.com

Acknowledgements

It would be impossible for me to list all of those individuals who have nurtured me during this journey of spiritual, emotional, and intellectual growth. I humbly offer this partial list of those who have supported me and my work for the last 20 years.

To my good friend Gene Ashely, I thank you for encouraging me to welcome these old friends and the gifts they have brought into my life and for challenging me to use the healing and psychic gifts latent within me. What a talented psychic you were. Harold Egelin, Jr., if it weren't for the support group, I'd be lost. To the late Dr. Jean Mundy and Brother Budd Hopkins, kudos to you both! To my mom and dad, William Carter and Rosetta D. Carter, I love you for allowing me to find my way without ridicule.

To my daughter Kevyn, you are the world to me. Annette, you've been such a great friend, kind, creative, insightful, constantly creating and recreating yourself, not to mention, you are an excellent editor. Dawn, what a gift you are to me, not to mention the energy of loyalty, humor, compassion, and love you bring to my life. I am eternally grateful to you and for you.

Last but certainly not least, I must acknowledge my friends, Octogon, Tandu, and Minyana; I thank you again for your cosmic love, guidance, humor, and companionship. I am eternally grateful.

About the Author

Rev. Michael J. Carter is originally from Baltimore, Maryland. He moved to New York City in 1980 and lived there for 27 years, working as a professional actor before moving to Asheville with his family.

Rev. Carter is an ordained Interfaith Minister and received his BA Degree in Letters from the College of New Rochelle, where he graduated cum laude. Rev. Carter received a Master of Divinity Degree from Union Theological Seminary in New York City (2000). Rev. Carter is also a Board Certified Chaplain (Retired).

While serving various Unitarian Universalist Congregations in New York, Michael was trained as an anti-racism trainer and earned recognition by President Clinton for his efforts.

Rev. Carter is the author of four books; *Alien Scriptures: Extraterrestrials in the Holy Bible, A New World If You Can Take It: God, Extraterrestrials and The Evolution of Human Consciousness, God Consciousness: A 30 Day Meditation Manual To God-Centered Thinking,* and *The Metaphysics of Spiritual Healing and the Power of Affirmative Prayer.*

A long-time Contact Experiencer, Rev. Carter lectures extensively on the topic of religion and UFOs. He is featured in the Sci-Fy Channel's Steven Spielberg's production of *Abduction Diaries,* The documentary film, *The Real 4400,* The Travel Channel's production of *UFOs: The Hidden Evidence,* and is a frequent guest consultant on The History's Channel's production, *Ancient Aliens,* including, *William Shatner meets Ancient Aliens.*

He currently serves as the minister for The Unitarian Universalist Congregation of The Swannanoa Valley, in the beautiful mountains of Western North Carolina.